THE NOBLE

BOATBUILDERS OF FRASERBURGH

MIKE SMYLIE

T0307415

THE NOBLE

BOATBUILDERS OF FRASERBURGH

MIKE SMYLIE

The
History
Press

Front cover image of the *Florentine* courtesy of Lachie Paterson.

First published 2022

The History Press
97 St George's Place, Cheltenham,
Gloucestershire, GL50 3QB
www.thehistorypress.co.uk

British Library Cataloguing in Publication Data.
A catalogue record for this book is available from the British Library.

ISBN 978 0 7509 9955 7

Typesetting and origination by The History Press
Printed and bound by TJ Books Limited, Padstow, Cornwall

Trees for LYfe

Christine, PD374, in Aberdeen. (Wilson Noble)

Florentine lying at Fraserburgh in 1932. (James Noble)

Silver Crest almost derelict before she
sank on Loch Ness. (James Noble)

Carrick Lass at Rye, as RX167, in about 1970. (James Noble)

Girl Irene, INS58, alongside at Lossiemouth. (James Noble)

Goldseeker. (James Noble)

CONTENTS

ᴵNTRODUCTION AND ᴬCKNOWLEDGEMENTS

Off I had set once again, hard on the heels of the success of the Tommy Summers book, to chronicle another of the boatbuilders of Fraserburgh. As I admitted in that first book (*Thomas Summers & Co. Boatbuilders of Fraserburgh*, published by The History Press in 2020), it was the determination of Malcolm Burge and Alexander West that drove the project on. This time not much had changed, which was why I was propelling myself north again once the pandemic restrictions had somewhat eased.

And so I arrive in Mallaig, that 'doyen' of the West Highland herring, and I find myself staring down at *Stella Maris*, PH97, ex-*Iris*, FR7, built by James Noble in 1968. She has that old withered look about her, tired wheelhouse and deck resulting from years of hard toil. My phone rings and it's my old mate Luke Powell, wooden boatwright extraordinaire, in Mallaig with his new-build *Pellew*, a replica of a Falmouth pilot boat. I spy her huge mast over the fishing boats, in among the plastic yachts in the marina.

Powell builds wooden boats with a vengeance and is largely responsible for the growth in new wooden craft. But he always teases me and this time is no exception.

'Why aren't you writing about getting people to build new fishing boats in wood rather than all that stuff about history?' He talks like he's lamenting the end of an era, which I guess is pretty close to the truth. He, along with a couple of others, doggedly refuse to give up on wood for the construction of 'working boats', even if their description of 'working' means 'chartering'. Yet, their new vessels prove that wood remains a viable material for large vessels and he wouldn't be the first boatbuilder to state categorically that they could build an under-10-metre for a price that matches steel.

So I prevaricate that I leave that sort of talk up to 'you boatbuilders', even if, in my heart, I know he's right. I look at some of today's steel new-builds and I see nothing of beauty of any description in them. Yet the curves and shape of a wonderful wooden fishing boat please almost everyone's eyes!

My own eye moves to the slipway, where I see *Prevail*, a wooden vessel that sank in Stornoway and was written off, ready to be unceremoniously dismantled until John Wood took her on to restore her as a working vessel. John has already reincarnated *Crimson Arrow*, KY142, ex-*Maureen*, WK270, built by Jimmy Noble, and was fishing her from Mallaig until a week before. Sod's law, I guess, that I'd missed her.

Powell's comments lie heavily on my mind as I travel north. Arriving at Isle Ewe boats, I can only feast on the sight of the Lochfyne skiff *Clan Gordon* under restoration, a vessel whose fortunes (and misfortunes) I've been following ever since I sold my own Lochfyne skiff *Perseverance*, CN152, to owners who then sank her in the Atlantic.

Then to Ullapool, where I find another vessel, *St Vincent*, 405CY, at the loch-side yard of Johnson & Loftus, being restored, both these being funded by the same source. Both were early builds (1911 and 1910 respectively) and both worked these West Highland waters.

Finally, and the whole reason for being here, I meet the Noble-built *Goldseeker*, the 1967-built fishery research vessel, financed by the Department of Agriculture and Fisheries for Scotland, to work mostly, I believe, along the west coast. She moved to private hands in 1993 and today is owned and kept in wonderfully tip-top fettle by Scott Coleman and Robyn Thegrate. Simply boarding her at Ullapool's pier, the boat instantly exudes its unique vintage, like a fine wine, so that I breathe in and imbibe! She truly is a gem, almost original except for some internals, complete with her original Gardner 6LX purring below.

We cast off and head out into the loch, viewing a couple of the wrecks along the coast, including the Tommy Summers' *Easter Morn*. Down to the lighthouse at Rubha Cadail before turning for home, just enough time to get the feel of her even if the sea is calm. When we part, I feel I know the boat for some weird reason. But it is enough and, with the usual tear when leaving the west coast, we head east. To the Broch then, where these workhorses started out and hopefully to the last remnants of the story that has been growing over the lost months of the pandemic …

As usual there are many people who have been instrumental in this book. First off have to be Alexander West and Malcolm Burge, who started the whole Facebook thing, and Malcolm for his continued work on it.

Then I must mention the Scottish Fisheries Museum, and Linda Fitzpatrick in particular, where most of the work detailing the lists for each yard was undertaken. Obviously here we are only talking about the Wilson and James Noble lists, but they've also completed the Tommy Summers and J. & G. Forbes ones.

Bill MacDonald, Benny Noble and Chris Reid from the Fraserburgh Heritage Centre, where the Tommy Summers book was launched just before this pandemic began to take hold of us, have been helpful. Bill MacDonald's 1992 book *Boats & Builders: The History of Boatbuilding Around Fraserburgh* has been vital in understanding these yards.

Noble family members have provided much background of the individuals in the firms. These are Wilson Noble junior's daughter, Maureen Small; Charlie Noble's sons, James and Charlie; and Maureen and Bruce Herd, Yankee's daughter and her husband.

For his memories of both yards (and Tommy Summers'), 88-year-old Bobby Jones was priceless, thanks to help from Crawford Rosie, who took me to meet him after I'd listened to various tales they had recorded together over the lost months of the pandemic. It really was a pleasure to meet you, Bobby!

To Alastair Noble of Girvan and his father Peter, who sadly passed away during the writing of this book, thanks for the family memories and connections.

For snippets of information, I mention Willie Whyte, Charles William Forbes, Jimmy and John May, Willie McRobbie, George Forbes, George Westwood, Fred Normandale, Simon Sawers and Mary Melville. Then Billy and John Wood for their information (and determination) on the restorations of *Crimson Arrow* and *Crimson Sea*.

To *Ocean Pearl*, whom I first met, thanks to Michael Custance and Nick Gates, many years ago.

To Scott Coleman and Robyn Thegrate for introducing me to *Goldseeker*.

To my daughter Ana for keeping me sane during our week-long trip around Scotland, and Luke Powell, Adrian Morgan and Rory MacPhee for sustenance during that trip. I'll add boatbuilders Alasdair Grant, Tim Loftus and Dan Johnson who understand these boats, simply because I can!

For photographs, first Lachie Paterson for sharing – no, drip-feeding – me a wee bit of the wealth of his extensive photo archive, and to Angus Martin for edging him along.

Family photos have come from Maureen Small (Wilson's) and Maureen and Bruce Herd (Jimmy's). Not to be omitted are Maureen Herd's brother, Martin McDonald, and his wife, for organising and transporting the family photos back to Scotland from Houston where they live.

Then Darren Purves for accessing some wonderful 1970s slides, as well as allowing me to use some of his own (and his son's!) photos. Finally Willie

Mouat, Finlay Oman and Peter Drummond, who kindly sent me some from their collections. Last of all, all users of the 'Wooden Boats by Wilson Noble' and the 'Wooden Boats by James Noble' Facebook sites, where the majority of the photos, along with snippets of information, have come from. It was widely publicised that they would be used in the book and several people came forward, and their photos acknowledged. Others have also been credited where the photographer is known. If there are omissions, for which I apologise, please contact the publisher so that this can be rectified in any future reprint.

Finally, my thanks to Amy Rigg at The History Press for her art of persuasion to get this book off the starting line, and the subsequent job to get it into anything resembling sense!

1

A Little Bit of History

Fraserburgh – originally an amalgamation of the harbour of Faithlie, first built about 1547, on the eastern side of the north-west tip of Aberdeenshire and the fishing village of Broadsea (originally Seatown) to the north-west around the bay – was laid out as a new town in the sixteenth century by the local landowning Fraser family of Philorth. Hence, Fraser's burgh or 'Frazersburgh', as one map-maker put it in 1747, a time after it had become a Royal Burgh in 1601. Built to compete with Peterhead and Aberdeen, it was initially the herring fishing, and subsequently the white fishery, that created the harbour (and town) as it is now. But it was Broadsea that was originally the home of the fishermen and, in 1789, it had forty-two working off the beach with small open boats, twenty-nine of whom were Nobles. There were seven boats crewed by six men in each, and they sailed as far as Barrahead in their search for fish.

Faithlie was little more than a couple of quays surrounding a sandy beach where boats could be drawn up and, prior to the nineteenth century, was the domain of soldiers and trading boats. Presumably it was exposed to the south-east. By the early nineteenth century the North Pier had been extended and the South Harbour added. This was a time when the herring fishing was expanding rapidly after Government intervention in the 1790s. Fraserburgh then became an important herring station during the early summer season and, presumably, the Broadsea men based themselves there.

By 1815 bounties for the herring fishing had been introduced for small craft and the east coast of Scotland's herring fishing turned from being a cottage industry to a commercial fishery. That year, as John Cranna tells us in *Fraserburgh, Past and Present*:

The boats had no decks whatever, and measured about 20 feet of keel and 12 feet of beam. The crews depended as much upon the oars as the sails for going to and coming from the fishing grounds. The craft never went more than a few miles from the shore in quest of the herring. This accounts for the comparatively small loss of life at sea in these early years. Caught in a gale thirty or forty miles at sea, these cockle shells would have instantly foundered, with results which need not be conjured up. The crews, however, excellent judges of the weather, kept the harbour when lowering clouds appeared, and if at sea, smelt danger from afar, and promptly sought the friendly shelter of port before the fury of the tempest overtook them. Thus were they able nearly a hundred years ago to prosecute their calling in comparative safety, frail though their boats were.

Further developments in the nineteenth century created a much larger harbour as the herring fishing flourished. The number of boats participating in the herring fishing in the district increased rapidly so that by 1830 there were 214 Fraserburgh boats, twenty-four from Peterhead and thirty-four from Rosehearty. This suggests that there were only local boats working out of the harbour, although Cranna reports that boats came from the Firth of Forth and a few from the north. At the same time, as Cranna mentions, there were thirty fish-curing yards dotted around the town:

> in the most out-of-the-way places. Messrs. Bruce, for instance, cured on a little bit of ground facing Broad Street and Shore Street, immediately to the south of the Crown Hotel. Curing plots were being freely let off at the entrance to the Links, about or near where the railway station now is, and several firms cured there. The trade was slowly but surely consolidating at Fraserburgh. In the year 1830 the catch of herrings in the Fraserburgh district, which included Peterhead, etc., touched the very respectable figures of 56,182 crans, while the number of curers for Fraserburgh alone was 30, being two more than in 1828.

Boat design was altered after the great south-easterly storm in August 1848, when many fishing boats were lost along the east coast and there were many fatalities among the fishers. Many were overcome by the sheer force of the waves when returning in the face of the storm to unsafe harbours, although it seems that the Fraserburgh men survived whereas in Peterhead there were thirty-one casualties and twenty-eight boats wrecked. The storm forced Parliament to act and the subsequent report submitted by Captain John Washington made various recommendations in regard to harbour improvement and vessel design, as well as the phasing out of plying fishermen with whisky in part payment for their labours! However, Fraserburgh did have its own storm to remember, in 1850, when a north-westerly gale forced boats onto the sands. Nevertheless, only one life was lost, with ten boats driven ashore.

In the harbour, the Balaclava Pier was added over the Inch Rocks in the 1850s to create more protection and later the South Pier was built, followed by the Balaclava harbour works. Boats also became larger due to improved building techniques in carvel construction, where planks are laid side by side instead of overlapping or clinker (clench) building. Decks were added to the previously undecked craft, affording greater seaworthiness and safety at sea.

As more and more men were enticed into fishing – what else was there? – the demand for fishing boats grew, as that for did trading vessels to carry the herring off to markets. With the arrival of the railway to Fraserburgh in 1865, allowing fish to be carried away to the centres of population such as Edinburgh and Glasgow, the landings increased rapidly. Some maritime industries suffered – sail-making and rope works in the main – as these commodities could be produced elsewhere cheaper, but Fraserburgh saw no incoming industrialisation on a large scale.

Fishing became the main occupation of the second half of the nineteenth century, aboard, at first, the great Zulus and fifies, with their powerful lug rigs, then with the introduction of steam drifters and trawlers. In the 1880s there were some sixty curers working in the town. On one night in July 1884, 667 boats landed 20,010 cran of herring, and the herring lassies were kept busy processing this catch into barrels. But such was the enormity of the catch, and the fact that the fish were small, that even though they worked all night, the women were unable to gut it all. With more being landed the next day, some 4,000 cran were dumped in the harbour and plenty more was carted to farmers, who laid it on their fields as fertiliser.

Fish processing (an improvement from 'curing'), an important part of the industry, supplied the British army with rations in the Boer War and again in both the First and Second World Wars. In the early 1920s, with the advent of the internal combustion engine, so began the last great development in wooden fishing boat design with cruiser-sterned herring drifters, canoe-sterned ring-netters, double-ended seiners, leading to, later, transom-sterned craft as motor power increased. Further harbour expansion brought about the Faithlie Basin, the completion of which ended the expansion of the harbour, although improvements continued and do so right up to this day.

Needless to say, the provision of boats needed boatbuilders and Fraserburgh has had some well-known names in that respect over time. One of the first documented was a Mr John Dalrymple, a member of a family that came to Fraserburgh from the Firth of Forth, who had a facility at Black Sands in the early nineteenth century. They, it is said, had seen an opening in the quickly expanding herring fishery.

Another was John Webster, described as a shipbuilder, who employed fifty carpenters and who commenced work in 1840 but had ceased by 1887. It appears he was originally from Aberdeen but chose Fraserburgh to set up his yard. Over this period he is said to have built at least fifty-seven vessels excluding local fishing vessels. His last boat was *Shiantelle*, built for renowned naturalist J.A. Harvie-Brown for his expeditions to the western and northern Scottish Isles for the years up to 1891.

Mr Weatherhead – a name well known further south – opened a facility in about 1884 in a location by the Kessock Burn, which would have been in the vicinity of today's Kessock Park. This appears to have been the first recorded yard in Fraserburgh devoted to the building of modern (of that era) fishing boats. However, the location of the premises Weatherhead worked in made launching boats difficult, given they had to be hauled over to the beach by horse. This yard had closed by the turn of the new century.

In 1890 two men, both of whom had been apprentices for Webster, took over his dilapidated yard and set themselves up as Scott & Yule. This company was, according to Cranna in 1914, 'kept very busy building fishing boats known as steam drifters, which in some measure, fills up the gap caused by the collapse of shipbuilding'. However, within a year the yard had closed – maybe a reflection of the general state of shipbuilding. Records supply us with details of at least eighteen steam drifters built between 1907 and 1915.

Broadsea man Alexander Noble had served his apprenticeship with Weatherhead's. When Scott & Yule took over Webster's, Alexander Noble was soon to join their workforce. Eight years later, in 1898, he decided he wanted to branch out on his own and set up a small boat repair yard at the foot of the Royal Hotel Brae. He was obviously well known locally and fishermen persuaded him, it seems, to commence boatbuilding, for which he needed larger premises. He moved to a yard in the Balaclava Basin, adjacent to the Provost Anderson's Jetty, where he launched the *Sincere*, FR909, for Robert Duthie in 1899. This was soon followed by the 70ft fifie *Victoria*, FR971, for Broadsea owners G. Noble & J. Buchan. *Victoria* was a successful boat and a story emerged that, as long as *Victoria* was sailing, the yard would continue to prosper.

Alexander, known as Cocky, was the son of Alexander, known as Auld Cocky. He married Elizabeth, whose maiden name was also Noble, and together they had eight children: Wilson, Alexander, James, Charles, Magdelene, Elizabeth and two others who died in childhood.

Despite initial success, in 1901, Alexander Noble handed over the running of the yard to his eldest son Wilson (sometimes also referred to as Cocky), whom he deemed was more interested in the business side of running a busy yard. Wilson had served his apprenticeship as a cabinetmaker in Fraserburgh, as had his younger brother Alexander, and both worked in the yard after their apprenticeships had concluded. Thus the name of the yard then became Wilson Noble & Co.

Two adverts for the consolidated Pneumatic Tool Co. Ltd (known locally as 'Toolies').

WILSON NOBLE & CO.

After Scott & Yule closed down in 1915, Wilson Noble & Co. was left as the only boatyard in Fraserburgh building fishing boats, while down the road in nearby Sandhaven, Forbes was successfully plying the same trade as it had since the 1880s. In 1902, George Forbes, the founder, handed over to his sons James and George and the name J. & G. Forbes was born. It was a name synonymous with fishing vessels up to the yard's closure in 1990, although Forbes did retain a repair yard in Fraserburgh harbour.

To recap, Wilson Noble had three brothers Alexander (b.1886), James (b.1891) and Charles (b.1893). He was the eldest, having some five years over his nearest brother, Alexander, and was married to Rachael Grant Cardno. Together they had four children: Wilson junior, Mary, Margaret and Alexander, known as Zander. Margaret and Zander were twins, while Wilson junior was the youngest of all.

Although Wilson – known locally as Cocky, as mentioned – and Alexander were running the yard, both James and Charles served their apprenticeships there. The early part of the twentieth century was a time of change in fishing boat

A dapper Wilson Noble with his wife, Rachael. (Maureen Small)

Rachael and Wilson Noble. (Maureen Small)

design. Such craft had grown in size in the latter part of the nineteenth century thanks to changes in techniques and the availability of heavier and longer
pieces of timber. Carvel construction, whereby planks are laid onto a backbone of
frames, superseded clinker construction in most larger craft. The advent of steam-
driven vessels demanded larger craft. In Fraserburgh and the surrounding area,
there were generally two types of sailing fishing vessel still working: the upright
fifie type and the more progressive and faster Zulu type. Both were considered
as immensely strong and seaworthy fishing vessels, used mostly in the pursuit of
herring, while smaller craft were working long-lines for white fish and creels
for shellfish. Steam-driven vessels were, for the moment, restricted to trawling
and drifting, although the Fraserburgh fishermen were slow to catch on. Thus
we believe that the first wooden steam drifter built in the harbour was in 1907.
Which yard was responsible is unclear but the first Noble-built steam drifter
was the 90ft *Gowan*, FR232, launched that year, followed by the slightly smaller
Kinnaird, FR205, later that year. That was in the days before the covered yard
was built. When the *Kinnaird* was launched, it is reported that part of the quay
was chipped away to facilitate the launch off the quayside. That year, between
the three Broch yards in operation – Wilson Noble, Scott & Yule and Forbes of
Sandhaven – Fraserburgh boatbuilders launched twelve steam drifters.

A few years later, in 1911, Wilson Noble launched two well-documented
sister ships: the small Zulus *Violet* (FR451) and *Vesper* (FR453). Although not as
long as the true first-class Zulu of the late nineteenth century, when such vessels were over 80ft long with massive overhangs at the stern, nonetheless both
these vessels were 45ft overall and have been termed 'half-Zulus'. A note of
caution: although I term them half-Zulus because, in my opinion, they are not
the larger first-class vessels and tend to only have one dipping lugsail whereas
the large craft had two massive sails on equally massive spars, there are those
who insist on the Zulu label for all vessels with a raking sternpost, angled at
some 45 degrees. Personally I disagree, believing the whole point of terminol-
ogy is to critically evaluate, and thus group, vessels of equal stature. Regardless,
they were both long-standing vessels and *Violet* survives to this very day in the
US (see Chapter 4: 'Some Survivors').

There are very few records of other boats built prior to the First World War,
although we can only assume that the yard was turning out a handful each year,
especially when fishing was booming. However, we do know that *White Oak*,
FR558, was launched in 1913 and *Violet Flower*, PD148, the following year,
before the outbreak of war. *Kinnaird* foundered in Loch Eport in 1930, and
Gowan and *White Oak* survived into the 1930s, whereas the 91.5ft *Violet Flower*
wasn't scrapped until 1947.

The family: L–R Wilson, Rachael, Mary, Margaret, Wilson junior and Alexander (Zander). (Maureen Small)

The family again in more formal stance. (Maureen Small)

During the war itself, although records are again scarce, we do know that Wilson Noble built at least ten steam-driven Admiralty vessels, and converted many more. Only details of two of these drifters remain: *Mackerel Sky* and *Milky Way*, both close to 90ft long. After the war, both went into fishing on the east coast until being scrapped in 1951. Presumably the others were similar in design. Three were completed after the end of hostilities in 1919–20, when there was a brief post-war boom in the fortunes of the harbour.

It was at this time that another Alexander Noble (though of no known family relationship) was brought to the yard at six o'clock one morning in 1919 by his fisherman father Peter Noble and was apprenticed to the yard under the guidance of Cocky. In his National Maritime Museum monograph (no. 31, 1978) entitled *The Scottish Inshore Fishing Vessel: Design, Construction & Repair*, this Alexander Noble notes that he was 14 at the time and that 'the firm employed about eighty men' on the Monday morning that he turned up for work. After serving his time, and perhaps a further spell in the yard, Alexander moved west in 1933 to take up a position as foreman in a yard in Killibegs, Ireland, before returning to Scotland four years later to work with James A. Silver, yacht builders at Rosneath. Part of his work was the repair and maintenance work on Clyde-based ring-net fishing vessels, some from the Girvan area. After almost a decade at Rosneath, Alexander, along with his son James, set up Alexander Noble & Sons Ltd of Girvan, a yard renowned for its fishing vessels and one still surviving, in part on fishing boat maintenance (see *Built by Nobles of Girvan* by Sam Henderson and Peter Drummond, published by The History Press, 2010).

Whether there is a blood connection between the Fraserburgh and Girvan Nobles still remains to be seen, even if we do know about the apprenticeship link. The Girvan Nobles have traced their ancestry back to another Alexander Noble, who was born in 1609 and lived at 84, Broadsea, Fraserburgh, and was still living in 1690. He became the first harbourmaster of Peterhead's harbour, where the initial construction of what is today's Port Henry Basin began in 1593. Common sense tells us that there's a good chance of a family connection in the intervening ten generations!

It is interesting also to note that Alexander Noble, in his monograph, mentions that he received thorough training in the building of all types of vessels, from fishing vessels to yachts and launches, using both clinker and carvel construction. This suggests that Wilson Noble was also building small yachts and clinker launches at that time, even if there's no record of these craft.

In the years following the war, with steam drifters being shunned in place of motorised vessels and new boats being fitted with engines, the design of boats surprisingly didn't change very much. Another built on Zulu lines in 1920, albeit a small one, was *Evangeline*, FR729, which survived until catching fire in Anstruther in about 2002. The same year they built *Village Maid*, TT26, which is listed as being for W. Noble of Fraserburgh. This we assume was Wilson Noble, building on spec, and it was later sold to Tarbert owners, the first of four *Village Maid*s to work from that harbour.

In 1922 Wilson won a contract to build *Corbiehill*, a 95ft drifter-style vessel intended for carrying empty herring barrels back to the curers. The cost to the Fraserburgh Shipping Company was £14,000 but, after two years, she was deemed to be unsuccessful at her intended purpose. The boat suffered many problems, although it is not known whether these were a result of her construction or design. Some £6,000 was spent on repairs and reconstruction but, even so, her owners ended up laying the vessel up in Lowestoft after she was towed into Great Yarmouth in a poor state and presumably without power. Consequently she was sold to a Duncan Sandison of Wick for £1,000. An article in the *Aberdeen Press & Journal* at the time stressed the loss in terms of the value of the vessel. Renamed *Millrock*, it appears she was then trading along the British east coast up to about 1931 and subsequently seems to have entered Norwegian ownership. By 1958 she had been renamed *Andvag* and the following year, on 23 December, she collided with M/S *Steinravn* while on passage from Oslo to Mosjøen loaded with iron and general cargo, and sank in Harøyfjorden, with the loss of two crew.

In the depression of the early 1920s – caused on the Broch as much by the disappearance of the herring export to Russia as by other international matters – fishing, and consequently fishing boat building, fell into the doldrums. Yet, even after laying off some of his workforce, Wilson managed to obtain orders for smaller inshore craft. These yoles, anywhere between 20 and 30ft long, were seldom listed in the yard's records, yet they became known as the Mosquito Fleet, such was their number. They were said to swarm like mosquitoes as they raced back from where they were setting their lines, to be the first to reach the 4 p.m. Fraserburgh market. They were all painted green to add to their swarm-like tendencies!

During the first half of the 1920s, apart from *Evangeline* and *Village Maid*, Wilson Noble only built six larger vessels up to 1925, an average of one and a half each year, all around 40ft long. Possibly there were some yawls that were never documented. After 1925 things obviously had improved, judging by the list of vessels, with nineteen produced between 1925 and 1929, seven of these in 1929 alone. Two of the 1926 vessels were of the motorised Lochfyne skiff type, 43.2ft long with Gleniffer motors, used for ring-netting out of Carradale, where

Wilson's boats continued in favour (and which carried on to James Noble). By this time the overall size was increasing, with at least two being over 50ft. In 1928 Wilson launched *Lindfar*, BK234, considered by some to be the first new-build diesel-engine vessel in the country, in contrast to the petrol/paraffin engines.

But the nature of fishing was changing rapidly, alongside developments in hull construction. Wilson Noble had been given the first electric drills from the Consolidated Pneumatic Tool Co. (C.P.T.) of London and Fraserburgh, to see how they fared on the construction of *Corbiehill*, for them later to go into mass production. Electricity came via generators. The main works for C.P.T. was in Fraserburgh, where it had opened for the production of pneumatic tools in 1906, which explains why Wilson Noble's was chosen to test the early electric drills. It was said that there were few folk in the Broch who did not have a connection to 'Toolies', as the company was known.

Thus, Wilson Noble & Co. entered the 1930s with a degree of optimism, although it has been said that, to begin with, the company suffered setbacks as well as successes. Orders were for smaller 35–45ft fifie-type vessels, often referred to as 'bauldies' in the sailing era, after the Italian patriot Garibaldi impressed the Scots fishers in the same way that they had admired the tenacity of the Zulu wars in South Africa, especially because thousands of Scots had died in battles that they regarded as caused by English colonialism. Hence the type of fishing boat referred to as a Zulu.

These small inshore boats, although similar to the older-type bauldies, had done away with the rig, and were fitted with engines and wheelhouses. One of these was the 45ft motorised bauldie *Harvest Reaper*, FR235, launched in 1931 for John Downie May of Fraserburgh. Costing £630, she had a small 30hp Kelvin and stayed within that family, with John's son Jimmy skippering her until 1974. Jimmy told me that she was as good a sea boat as there ever was, 'a grand boat'. He lamented her sale and reckoned he passed her on too cheaply. She was replaced by a Jimmy Noble boat, another *Harvest Reaper*, FR177, in 1975.

In 1934 Wilson launched the *Briar*, FR48, a 55.6ft vessel for William Buchan of Fraserburgh, complete with a canoe stern. This was regarded as something new for a vessel of this size, although the smaller ring-netters had such lines since the previous decade. *Briar* was designed as a dual-purpose seiner/herring drifter, a sign that the Danish seine net was beginning to take precedence over the herring fishery, which was in serious decline. Built at an overall cost of £1,200 with a Kelvin K3 66hp (hull £500, engine £600 and gear £100), she was found to be underpowered, so the engine was changed for an 88hp K4 Kelvin. This boat proved herself in all sorts of weather and attracted interest from other owners. Wilson suddenly had a full order book.

The *Briar* continued working until being sold to Grimsby in 1977 and she soon came under the ownership of the Halstead family of Hull. After fishing with her for a while and not making a success of it, they converted her to a gaff ketch and immigrated to Australia, crossing the Atlantic, passing through the Panama Canal and sailing via Tahiti and Fiji to reach Brisbane.

Wilson's younger brother, James, left in 1932 to set up his own yard. This was the beginning of James Noble & Co. in buildings at the end of the harbour, the Balaclava Inner Harbour. His brother Charles joined him and became the yard foreman. It seems that James had decided that concentrating on yacht building was the way forward, given the slump in fishing boats. How wrong he was, and before long he was building fishing boats, of which we will learn more in the next chapter.

At some point Wilson's son, also Wilson, joined the workforce. He had been born in 1919, so I'm supposing it would have been a bit before the Second World War, possibly just after James departed. Although Wilson senior's son, it seems he never had a control in the overall management of the yard. According to his daughter Maureen, who lives in New Zealand, her father was skilled when it came to working as a boatbuilder/carpenter but had no head for figures at all. 'I can't imagine him doing paperwork,' she told me.

It was not long after, in 1939, that an excerpt in the *Edinburgh Gazette* tells us that George Noble had resigned as a partner in the business and that Wilson and Alexander Noble continued as the only subscribers to the company, the name Wilson Noble & Co. remaining the same. Where George came into the business to begin with remains unclear, as is any family connection, just as we don't know his reason for leaving. Perhaps he simply retired!

Boats were launched straight off the quay as the yard had no proper slipway before the war. However, after the war, a slipway was built that had to be covered up so that the road along the front of the yard could be used by vehicles. This road was allowed to be closed for three days prior to a launch and one day after, to allow opening up of the slipway.

That same year, 1939, the company built four fishing vessels, including the 69ft *Dundarg*, FR121, for the Duthie family of Rosehearty, and this still sails. There's a superb photograph of her launch over the quay with around twenty people clasping for life on the starboard bow. The launch obviously attracted a huge audience of locals.

Dundarg cost in the region of £3,000 to build, complete with engine and gear, and was launched by Mrs Duthie, wife of the skipper. The vessel managed one trip to the East Anglian herring fishery before the Second World War broke out, and she was soon requisitioned by the Admiralty. That year Wilson

Noble also built *Briar Rose*, FR67, another successful local boat that continued working up to the 1970s. The very same year the yard received the first order for a minesweeper from the Admiralty, now that war was a reality.

Thus both Wilsons continued working side by side, Wilson senior, alongside his brother Alexander, in charge of the office and Wilson junior running the yard. Wilson junior's elder brother, Zander, also worked there, though Maureen isn't sure in what capacity. 'I know he was there,' is all she said.

Throughout the war the building for the Admiralty continued at pace, as it did for all the Broch builders. Whereas James Noble was building 75ft motor fishing vessels (MFVs), Wilson was engaged in the production of what are called 110ft standard minesweepers, which actually measured 105ft between perpendiculars and 114ft overall, with a 165-ton displacement, between 1939 and 1943.

These vessels were designed of a simple construction so that the small yards used to building fishing vessels would be easily capable of adapting their workforce. Some 308 of these vessels were built during the war, some in the UK and others in Canada, India, Ceylon (Sri Lanka), Burma (Myanmar), Jamaica, Beirut (Lebanon) and Tel Aviv (Israel). Those remaining after the war were sold off and today the only known remaining vessel is *Lady Mack* (MMS173), converted to sail and working in Norway. It is said that some seventy-four of these vessels were imported into Scandinavia.

Then, in 1944, Wilson Noble built three of the larger standard 140ft minesweepers, which measured just under 140ft overall. Albert Ogston remembers how the stern of these boats stretched almost across Shore Street, the road at the rear of the yard. He also recalls how the harbour was wired off all along the promenade. Charles William Forbes notes that the building of these larger minesweepers 'shows in no small measure the contribution these small yards and their workforce were making to the war effort'. So true.

Security had been obviously pretty strict during the war and the companies were not supposed to keep records of what they built. Luckily, though, some records did survive so that we know that all three yards were engaged in Admiralty work.

Once the war effort had changed to chasing the German army into its own borders, the building of wooden minesweepers ceased and, over 1945 and 1946, Wilson Noble built a succession of the standard 75ft MFVs. After the cessation of hostilities these were sold off to fishermen, who received generous loans and grants. Many of the old steam drifters were left as rotting hulks on various shores. Yards were kept busy converting the Admiralty vessels for fishing and J. & G. Forbes opened their yard in Fraserburgh harbour for this very purpose.

Wilson Noble was the first to receive an order for a new vessel so that, in 1947, he launched the *Palm Tree*, FR43, as a copy of the successful *Briar*. Another such vessel was *Hazael 3*, FR107, launched in 1947.

In December 1966 *Hazael 3* was returning home for Christmas from fishing the west coast, based at Ullapool. Steaming through the Pentland Firth, near Holborn Head she collided with the 53ft seiner *Gleaners II* from Keiss. The vessel badly holed on her port side, skipper David Tait made straight for Scrabster, where they were heading for anyway because of bad weather. With the pumps running flat out, and the decks awash with water, they managed to make the harbour and once alongside the crew had to rush ashore just before the vessel sank in 2 fathoms of water. The skipper had decided he'd beach her if he wasn't able to make the harbour. Happily the vessel was later refloated and repaired.

Many equally fine vessels were built over the following years, into the mid-1950s, some even saying that these 70–75ft dual-purpose boats were Wilson's finest. A 70-footer, such as *Brighter Hope*, FR317, for instance, cost about £12,500, with finance through Government loans and grants available. Although, strangely maybe, there are no records of vessels being built in 1950, over the next five years the yard launched fourteen such craft, with one being for the Admiralty. Influence from building so many of these well-designed Admiralty vessels during the war must have come to bear on the subsequent boats Wilson designed.

Then, in 1956, completely out of the blue, Wilson senior died aged 75. This coincided with a decline in the fortunes of fishing, given the drop in herring landings, so fishermen had to rely solely upon those boats seining to cover their costs.

Alexander continued running the office side of the business but the writing was on the wall. Over the next two and a half years the yard only built three vessels, averaging one each for 1956, 1957 and 1958. With the younger Wilson having no head for business, seemingly happy working as a skilled carpenter, and Alexander nearing retirement age, there was no one wanting to run the yard. However, it did come as a bit of a surprise to the Fraserburgh fishing community when Wilson Noble & Co. ceased trading in 1959 and Wilson, his wife Jessie and their three daughters immigrated to New Zealand. Maureen remembers they loaded up their Morris Minor and drove to Southampton where, three days later, on 25 June 1959, they sailed for a new life. Wilson's Uncle Alec (Alexander) Noble died just a few months after Wilson had departed. Wilson himself continued working as a carpenter on the other side of the world, yet it must have seemed more than a world apart for someone brought up in the

Wilson addressing the haggis on Burns Night. (Maureen Small)

Alexander and Wilson senior in the boatyard. (Maureen Small)

world of fishing boat building on the Broch. He died in 1996.

Coincidentally, although Wilson probably would not have been aware of it, at least three of his vessels sailed 'down under', two (*Harmony*, FR416, in 1962 and *Silver Spray*, FR226, in 1964) to New Zealand and *Briar*, FR48, to Brisbane, Australia, in the early 1980s.

For superstitious readers, it's worth mentioning that the old 70ft fifie *Victoria*, FR971, built back in 1899, and said to survive as long as the yard did, was indeed involved in a collision in 1959. This occurred off Rosehearty with another Broch vessel *Iris*, FR322,

Alexander Noble. (Maureen Small)

Victoria, FR971, the boat that local superstition said would last as long as the Wilson yard existed.

and *Victoria* managed to stay afloat long enough to sail back to Fraserburgh. However, she was refused entry into the harbour due to the fact she looked as if she would sink imminently. Thus she was abandoned on the beach around Kinnaird Head, where she eventually broke up.

But the story of the yard doesn't quite end there for, a year after closure, Tommy Summers took it over and launched *Bdellium*, FR185, in 1961 and *Guiding Star*, LH382, later the same year. However, when Tommy ceased trading in 1962, the yard finally came to a complete standstill.

James Noble & Co.

As we have seen, James served his apprenticeship in his father's yard, as did Charles, possibly under his brother Wilson, who was ten years older than James, who himself was two years older than Charles. Alexander, who remained with Wilson throughout, was the second eldest. I'm assuming that through the First World War all four were engaged in boatbuilding rather than being at the front, though I've not come across any historical documentation to support this. Presumably they continued thus through the post-war period and the 1920s. By the 1930s all four brothers were married: Wilson to Rachael Grant Cardno, Alexander to Mary Elizabeth Noble, James to Jessie Jane Hendry and Charles to Isabella Thomson. Two sisters were also married: Magdelene to William Laird and Elizabeth to Thomas May.

Why James decided to split from his elder brothers isn't clear and probably the full truth of the matter never will be, but we can surmise that it was partly down to the after-effects of the slump in the fortunes of fishing. In the early 1930s, James seemingly lost all faith in the future of fishing boat construction and saw the building of yachts as where the path ahead lay. He was keen on expanding this and so broke away. The result was that he opened his own yard in 1932, and soon after his brother Charles joined him as yard foreman. He set up his yard at the north end of the breakwater, in the Balaclava inner harbour, not far from where Wilson's yard was on the western edge of the Balaclava harbour itself. For two years, no yacht building came the yard's way. Nevertheless, in that first year, it did build five fishing boats: *Wistaria*, BCK116, *Florentine*, CN197, *Cluaran*, CN240, *Alban*, CN242, and *Amy Harris*, CN249, so James had no reason to be envious of his brother Wilson, even if they weren't the yachts he'd hoped for. Part of his initial success seems to have been the way he managed to cut costs.

Bobby Jones reckons he built just a few yachts in the early 1930s: 'They only built two or three yachts, must have been in the mid-1930s because the herring fishing just took a nose drive. They were coming in every night and dumping it in the bay. There was a lot of carpenters at the time, older carpenters, things were so bad there were carpenters, tradesmen with no work and they finished up going to sea.'

At just over 40ft, *Wistaria* was built for J. Flett of Findochty, and other than the fact that she was sold to Fleetwood in 1938, little is known about her. But it was the building of *Florentine* for Carradale owners on the west coast that really started up the James Noble yard. At about 48ft, she was built for the ring-net, with a low freeboard, a varnished pitch pine hull and teak wheelhouse. Her owner was Walter MacConnachie of Carradale and she cost £850.

James was 41 when he started up his own business in 1932, so he must have had contacts within the fishing trade. Even so, it is intriguing to know how he gained his first few commissions. With *Florentine*, according to John MacConnachie, it was through his brother-in-law Jamie Campbell, who had parted company with his long-term neighbour at the ring-net and had suggested that they become partners. Jamie had had his boat *Irma*, CN45, built by Wilson Noble in 1929, so was keen to give the new yard an order. It seems that *Florentine* so impressed others back in Carradale, when she arrived in September that year, that the Galbraith family immediately ordered three other ringers – *Cluaran*, CN240, *Alban*, CN242, and *Amy Harris*, CN249. The following year James Noble produced another five for Carradale, as well as two for local owners and another to Arbroath. You could say this was instant success. Asking around, it became obvious that there were several reasons why fishermen used James Noble: the limited number of boatyards building fishing boats at the time; the boats were judged to be well built; they were good sea boats; and finally 'the price was right'.

At the same time, James Noble mirrored what was also happening at his brother Wilson's yard: building several small motorised bauldie types, which were still in demand. Thus the yard launched *Ocean Pearl*, FR378, and *Sincerity*, AH39, in 1933, both just under 40ft, double-ended with a sloping sternpost in the fifie/bauldie style. *Ocean Pearl* has since been restored and converted back to sail, and her longevity is as much a testament to her builders as it is to her restorer and present owner, Nick Gates, who keeps her in tip-top condition.

But word of James' desire to build yachts must have spread widely for in 1935 he was approached by letter by James Barnett, a director of the world-renowned yacht designer G.L. Watson Co. Ltd, to build a gentleman's motor yacht. You can just imagine his excitement at being approached, and the resultant yacht *Sheemaun*, built for banker Ernest Richards of Matlock, Derbyshire, continues to sail under the ownership of Rodney Peel, who has written a book dedicated to this most enduring of vessels (see *Little Ship, Big Story* by Rodney Peel,

The Conrad Press, 2019). There's a lovely description of how James Noble stuffs the unopened letter in his pocket as he leaves the yard and walks in the cold and wind to his homely cottage, with Jessie ready with a cup of tea, only to find the letter blown out of his pocket by the gale and onto the floor, which, to his joy, he then opens. There was possibly some artist licence, as James didn't live in a cottage, but nevertheless the incident reads as part of a long story of a worthy survivor.

Nearly all the ringers were built to a similar specification; all were around 48ft and engined generally with Kelvins. Some went to Ayrshire owners as James Noble's reputation spread around the ring-net fleets of the Clyde. As the 1930s drew to a close, lengths increased by a couple of feet, and even as the war years intervened, the company still managed to launch three vessels in 1940, including the 66ft *Flora Fraser*, FR181, the biggest vessel so far, for J. Ritchie of Fraserburgh. She was named after Marjorie Flora Fraser, the 8-year-old future Lady Saltoun of Philorth, daughter of the then Lord Saltoun, the local hereditary laird whose family had invested in the town (hence Fraserburgh!) over the centuries. The vessel was requisitioned for war use immediately after handover.

Perhaps that was a sign of things to come for over the next five years James Noble & Co. produced twenty-one Admiralty-class MFVs, at first the 50ft version and later the larger George Forbes-designed 75-footers.

It is said that timber supplies after the war were hard to come by, especially teak and pitch pine, and that James Noble had to turn to larch and Oregon pine to continue building his ring-netters. Sizes increased, as seen in the first post-war vessel, *Spindrift*, OB139, at 53ft overall, which went to Mallaig in 1946. Fast in her wake came *Mary Manson 2*, OB155, and *Primrose*, OB172, to join the Mallaig fleet. James Noble's launched seven that year and only the *Catherine & John*, DO21, was under 50ft. Ten followed the following year, eleven in 1948 and eight in 1949. Hulls were taking somewhere in the region of two months to complete in the shed, which is fast going by any standard, and then up to three months when fitting out in the harbour. Both Gardners and Kelvins alike were generally the skippers' choices of engine, with a couple of exceptions.

At least six ring-netters went to Avoch owners and others to various ports on the east coast, even if the majority of ring-netting was occurring on the west coast. At the same time, James received orders for long-liners that worked the cold and wild expanses of water as far north as Iceland. These – *Dainty Lady*, H509, and *Liberty*, H580 – both went to Bridlington owners in 1948, and were registered at Hull. The imaginatively named *Elizabeth Taylor*, H107, followed in 1950. Both *Dainty Lady* and *Elizabeth Taylor* were identical at 54ft, so I do wonder whether the owners were trying to say something! Unfortunately, *Elizabeth Taylor* was sunk only a year after her launch.

The 1940s workforce.

The workforce in 1957.

It was in 1948 that three of James Noble's workforce, Thomas Summers, George McLeman and Bill Duthie, realised there was a boom in fishing boat building and sensed an opening for another yard in Fraserburgh. They began work on their own behalf upon what was known as the Steamboat Quay, an exposed quayside open to the elements of the North Sea, building, to begin with, small yawls for the Broch fleet. All had been apprenticed at the boatyard and they were incredibly successful for over a decade. Their story is told in my earlier book, mentioned in the introduction, *Thomas Summers & Co. Boatbuilders of Fraserburgh*. Evidence suggests that, coincidentally, George McLeman was the nephew of Girvan-based Alexander Noble. Another small coincidence is that Tommy Summers' father, also Tommy, had had the 59ft *Venus Star*, FR223, built at James Noble's in 1936.

The workforce in 1958, celebrating with beer after a launch. *Back row:* Charlie Forbes, who worked in the yard for thirty-three years; Jimmy Duthie; Bob Masson, joiner; George Hutchison, joiner; Jimmy (Yankee) McDonald, joiner and co-owner; Charlie (Charlicky) Noble; Micky Hutcheson, carpenter; Billy (Berkie) Mitchell, apprentice carpenter; McPherson, labourer; James Strachan, apprentice carpenter; Charlie Noble, carpenter, sawyer and Jimmy Noble's brother. *Middle row:* two engineers, one named Yule; John Crawford, carpenter; Andrew May, apprentice carpenter; Johny Walker, apprentice carpenter; Charlie Noble senior, carpenter; Topper Noble, carpenter; Stough, store man. *Front row:* unknown; Johnnie Dunbar, carpenter; Jimmy Ritchie, carpenter; unknown; unknown young boy; Jimmy Noble, the boss; Johnnie Fae of Rosehearty, store man; Bobby Christie, apprentice carpenter; Charlie Forbes, apprentice carpenter. (Names thanks to George Forbes)

Thus James Noble continued to produce vessels in the 45–65ft range throughout the 1950s, albeit at a reduced rate from the 1940s. Some were seiners for Lossiemouth owners, the last in 1960 being the larger *Wave Sheaf*, INS118, at 68.2ft. English owners accounted for many orders through the period from the mid-1950s into the next decade, with four based in Newlyn, four 49ft Danish-style seiners into Hartlepool and one, *Margaret Jane*, SH17, into Scarborough. The latter was in 1957, when the yard still managed to launch eight fishing vessels. By that time the large main shed had been built for the construction of the yard's last Admiralty order of another 75-footer – MFV1254. Whether this structure had been an Admiralty requirement or simply the result of a high-priced commission is unclear.

By this time the yard was being run by Charles Noble's two sons, James (Jimmy) and Charles (Charlie), because James and Jessie Jane Hendry never had any children. When James retired in the late 1950s, Jessie took a controlling interest in the yard, even though Charles continued to run it. James died in 1959 and, when Jessie then died in 1975, she left the bulk of her estate to Jimmy (Yankee) McDonald.

This Jimmy got his nickname of 'Yankee' from the fact he was born in Detroit in 1928. His mother Helen (Nel) was Jessie Jane Hendry's sister and she, obviously pregnant, and her husband James (Lachie) McDonald immigrated to the US the same year but, with the slump, had to return in 1933. Being homeless, Jimmy and his brother stayed with his aunt and uncle for a while before the house was split, with the McDonalds living upstairs in the house while James and Jessie were downstairs. Thus Yankee (and I use this term forthwith to avoid confusion) became almost a son to the Nobles, having the best of both worlds when he chose. Yankee went on to serve his time in the yard and, unsurprisingly, inherited when Jessie Jane died, thus obtaining the controlling interest. However, he continued working and ran the joinery shop, where he was described as being a 'perfectionist' in his finishing work. He did pass some shares over to both the younger Jimmy and Charlie, yet maintained his majority shareholding, and all three were directors. Jimmy Noble continued to run the yard with Charlie as foreman. On the other hand, although he had worked in the yard through most of his working life, Charles senior never had any share in the business. Jimmy Noble had joined the yard soon after the war, after he'd been captured and had spent time in a prisoner-of-war camp. Charlie joined soon after.

Coincidentally, Yankee's brother, John Hendry McDonald (known as Ian), served his apprenticeship as an engineer in the Broch and later returned to Detroit, founding and running a successful precision engineering company for the remainder of his working life.

Of the four Hartlepool vessels, two, *Fiona Fay*, HL113, and *Castle Eden*, HL115, were part-owned by William John Cook, who never went to sea but had shares in numerous boats, alongside his father and other merchants on Hartlepool's fish quay. Given that these vessels were all almost identical – length overall 49ft, beam 19ft, depth 9ft and gross registered tonnage (GRT) approximately 24 tons and fitted with Gardner 5LW engines rated at 95hp – it is assumed that he probably also had shares in all these boats. Thus the list was *Kristiona* (built 1957), *Avondale* (built 1958), *Fiona Fay* (built 1958) and *Castle Eden* (built 1958).

From 1960 the numbers of launches decreased somewhat until 1969, when numbers were back up to six vessels for that and the subsequent year. Meanwhile, the yard had been gaining orders for small ferries for the inter-island short hops on the west coast and, over a period of a couple of decades, from the early 1950s to the late '60s, it built some fifteen ferries. One of the first was the 1951-built *Mamore*, which worked the short Kylesku to Kylestrome crossing. She had a revolving deck section to enable vehicles to drive on and drive off at an angle as she came alongside the slipway. In 1967 she was replaced by another Noble build, the *Queen of Kylesku*. She survived until being replaced by the Ardrossan-built *Maid of Glencoul* and then was stationed on the Corran to Ardgour crossing at the Corran Narrows on the Loch Linnhe crossing. Only one of these revolving turntable ferries remains today on the Glenelg to Kylerhea crossing to Skye, although not built by Noble's.

Once decommissioned as a ferry, *Mamore* was bought by Jimmy Young of Lochinver, who registered her for fishing as UL107. However, being totally flat-bottomed and shallow-drafted, she was wholly unsuited and, apart from one or two unsuccessful attempts at ring-netting, she was moored up near the pier in Lochinver until later rotting away on the side of the road between Lochinver harbour and the old Culag bridge – pretty much under where the new bridge is now.

One of the last ferries was the *Lochaber*, also for the Corran to Ardgour crossing, while at least another two went to the Ballachulish crossing of Loch Leven. The company even built several banana barges for the Dominican Republic in 1957. Along with some smaller yawls, the ferries, barges and various larger fishing craft, the yard survived the slump of the 1960s, and, as mentioned, increased its fishing boat output. In 1962 it even built a small 29ft open Yorkshire coble for Filey. However, I'm informed that when this vessel arrived by train at Filey, the owner deemed the stern not to be the required shape and it was sent back to Fraserburgh by train to have this rectified. Even so, it has been said that this was a pretty decent coble.

But fishing vessel design was marching on as trawlers were requiring a change in shape as engine power increased. When Noble's launched the 55ft new-style trawler *Maureen*, WK270, for Thurso owners in 1963, it proved to be very successful. With orders over the next few years, up to 1970, the yard produced six similar trawlers for Bridlington owners and three for Scarborough, along with some ten others for Scottish owners. Interestingly, some of the English owners retained the Fraserburgh registry to save the cost of re-registering them, though they always stayed working from their own bases. All were under 60ft as trawling in the inshore waters was only allowed by such vessels.

The end days of the cruiser-sterned fishing vessel were fast approaching in the mid-1960s. With increased engine power needed, more buoyancy aft as well as increased deck space for working over the stern, the transom stern soon dominated. James Noble built his first square-sterned boat in 1966, this being the 64.5ft *Argo*, FR255, which is said to have been a bit of a copy of the first Forbes-built square-sterned *Constellation*, FR294, the previous year. *Argo* had been designed by the Rev. E. Milton, minister at Rosehearty, an ex-naval architect and good friend of the owner R. Smith. She had her wheelhouse and engine forward, which gave a large working platform aft. Initially she was fitted with a whaleback to protect the wheelhouse from the waves, though it was removed soon after as it was deemed to affect the stability of the vessel.

The beginning of the 1970s saw big changes in the way boats were built. Naval architects were required to design boats, rather than the age-old method of the yard building a half model and having a commission based on that, with probably a few sketches on the back of fag packets! Both the White Fish Authority and the Herring Industry Board demanded certain requirements in building, such as all timber having to be racked for at least nine months to ensure proper drying out before use. Furthermore, safety regulations were being brought in, such as increased height of the handrails to ensure greater safety on deck. Not only was the timber being checked for quality, but now there were guarantees that the vessels were constructed in a proper way. Much of the demand for safety came after several craft were lost, the most high-profile being the sinking of the 2-year-old trawler *Gaul*, H243, in 1974. At the same time, engine power was overtaking the 200hp level and new companies had already moved into the sector that had previously only accommodated Gardner and Kelvin. Technology brought advances such as various navigating systems, especially Decca Navigation, echo sounders, radar and radio requirements. Stability tests became mandatory for all new vessels, while crew comforts also improved. For Jimmy Noble, this meant relying upon drawings for each boat, rather than just his eye. Previously, it appears, the moulds were made almost by eye and Bobby Jones recalls how, when they were fitting the sheer strake plank, Jimmy was always at hand to eye this in. He would say 'up an inch' or whatever just to suit each vessel, before the top strake was fixed. This was always oak, then, moving down, there was one in larch, another in oak, another in larch and the last in oak before the rest of the vessel, especially the underwater section, was planked in larch. In the latter years the topsides were all of oak. I asked Bobby about the machinery in the yard:

> We had a bandsaw to cut frames. Originally you had the wood that lay around the yard all laid out and Joe Strachan would come and draw the shape out. Labourers would come in with double-handed crosscut saws and cut to sizeable pieces and the squad took them to the bandsaw and you'd be three days cutting frames. Maybe more if it was a double-framed boat. It was a bandsaw that was made for boat frames: either they had a table that bevelled and others with a saw that bevelled. Tommy Summers had one where the table bevelled, and at Jimmy's it was the saw that tilted. Jimmy had a circular saw, a planer/chipper and electric drills; with pneumatic drills compared to what they have now. And a steam box; especially with those cruiser sterns, you needed it. Timber came cut into slabs. Great big loads used to lie along the breakwater while it was left a year or two. You'd see the timber coming, in the lorry, and you said, 'Right boys, we've another one to build here!'

There is a short film on YouTube by George Forbes of the tilting bandsaw in use cutting frames in J. & G. Forbes' yard in Sandhaven. Of course, there was none of today's health and safety rules, with bare hands pulling and pushing the 3 or 4in-thick oak slabs through the blade. The rest of the film shows the building of the last wooden vessel at the yard, which is fascinating in its own right.

For engineering, the Gardner agent in Fraserburgh was John S. Pirie, a company started up in 1938 and one that is still very much in existence looking after today's fishing fleet. It undertook all the Gardner installations while Joe Taylor, the Kelvin agent, was responsible for those engines. Between the two of them they managed the installation of any of these newcomers such as Caterpillar, as they had previously with Lister and Thornycroft. Northern Engineering fabricated all the steelwork in its shed next door to the yard.

Orders continued for the yard into the 1970s and vessels were not confined either way: cruiser sterns or transoms. The yard managed up to four a year, reducing to two in 1975 and then one in 1977, although it must be remembered that, given the increased work in these more modern vessels, they took much longer to complete. You wouldn't build one of those in a month! This was also reflected in the cost of the vessels, which had greatly increased to around £100,000 in 1970.

In 1971 the company launched its last but one cruiser-sterned vessel, *Jann Denise*, FR80, the last being *Silver Gem*, INS61, built in 1972. *Jann Denise* had been commissioned by Scarborough fisherman Gordon Pickering but tragically, in the meantime, he was lost at sea in an accident aboard *Ocean Gift*, PZ16, another Jimmy Noble boat. It had been intended that she be called *Mary Ellen* but, after Gordon was lost his good friend, Bob Walker was offered her and so he to,k her and named her *Jann Denise* after his own young daughter.

I discovered a little bit more about this boat from George Westwood. George told me she was sister ship to the Noble's boat *Eastern Dawn*, FR82, and was launched on 3 March 1971. It appears that she was supposed to have been launched on 1 March but Jimmy Noble would never launch any vessel on St David's Day, thus delaying the launch. However, I've not found any Welsh connection.

According to George:

She was kept in immaculate condition during her time at Scarborough and looked as if she had just left Noble's yard when she left Scarborough almost thirty years later. She did have the misfortune of being run down at night by a German coaster from Brake with her gear down and was saved only by the boxes of ice in the fish room, which prevented her from imploding.

Today she continues to fish and has been owned by Domhnall MacLachlainn since 2005, currently based in Peel, Isle of Man.

Jimmy May, whom readers might recall as owning the Wilson Noble-built *Harvest Reaper*, commissioned a new 55ft *Harvest Reaper*, FR177, which was launched in 1974. He described Jimmy Noble as 'fearsome', although he did add that, when Jimmy and his wife came round to discuss the build, Jimmy polished off a bottle of whisky and his wife almost a whole bottle of brandy. But that wasn't regarded as unusual then, and negotiations might go on for some time. It wouldn't be the first time I've heard of boatbuilders, even these days, who are able to drink in this way and handle it and, indeed, thrive on it. Jimmy May recalls that the boat cost him about £75,000 and he says the choice of using the yard was an easy one, given its reputation. However, he admitted, 'She wasn't as good a boat as the first *Harvest Reaper*.' He has an absolutely superb 25:1 scale model of her, after the shelter deck was fitted, in his front room.

During a period of lull in the mid-1970s, Noble's also took on the fitting out of the Swedish-built *Ocean Harvester*, N273, after the Swedish yard had shut down. While orders were low, the company had to look in other directions to keep going, and thus won contracts for the various ferries. Another of these part-builds was the 1976-launched *Dutch Bank*, K292, which had been partially built by J. Anderson (Boatbuilders) Ltd, Stromness. That yard in Orkney had previously, under the ownership of Pia Anderson, been well known for its fishing vessels, although when Pia died at the young age of 51 in 1971, the yard eventually went into receivership and Noble's won the contract to complete this vessel.

In 1977 Jimmy received an order from Fred Normandale for *Independence*, FR196, a 59ft boat. She was the only Noble-built vessel not actually built in Noble's yard. At the time, the Balaclava Basin was cofferdammed for deep dredging to allow the newer deep-drafted purse seiners to berth. So Jimmy Noble, with permission from the Harbour Commissioners, built her on the Paint Slip throughout the winter of 1976–77. Timbers were steamed in the Buchan, Hall & Mitchell steam box, which still lies alongside the yard there.

I asked Fred why he'd chosen Jimmy Noble and his answer was purely because he was going with the theory that they were a tried, tested and trusted yard by his peers. He was only 27 in 1975 when he commissioned *Independence*. His peers were the Mainprize family, although he stresses he is not part of that family. But, before that, back in 1957, when Tom 'Denk' Mainprize had ordered *Margaret Jane*, SH17, this was the start of a long association with Noble's and the Mainprize family. In Fred's own words:

> Denk subsequently built *Good Intent*, FR47, his son Larry had *Carol Ann*, SH175, in 1968 and then *Piscean*, FR276, in 1980, while Bobby Mainprize commissioned *Pathfinder*, FR172, in 1974 and a second *Margaret Jane*, FR297. Then Denk's son-in-law, Colin Jenkinson, built *Our Rachel*, FR97, in 1972, and then *Our Heritage*, FR237, in 1976.

That's quite a collection from one family. *Our Heritage* became a top earner in Scarborough and was a very popular vessel over the years.

Fred writes about *Independence* in his book *Slack Water* (Bottom End Publishing, 2004). With no connection to the Mainprize family other than friendship, he was invited to go to Fraserburgh for the launch of *Our Heritage*, where he met Jimmy Noble, though he'd been to the launch of *Jann Denise*, FR80, four years earlier.

At the time he owned the 54ft *Courage*, SH63, and he'd obviously been thinking about building his own boat because, being so impressed with what he saw in the yard, he went home and got in touch with the White Fish Authority. The upshot was that, with a quote from Jimmy Noble for £160,000, the WFA would give him a grant for a quarter of the cost and loaned him half the price

Launch (from left, back row: 1st, Charlie Noble snr; 2nd, Jimmy McDonald; 5th,
Jimmy Noble jnr; 6th, Jimmy Noble snr; and 1st from right, Mrs Jimmy Noble jnr.
Front row, from left: 1st, Mrs Charlie Noble snr; 7th, Mrs Jessie Noble; 9th, Mrs
Jimmy McDonald; 10th, Bessie Campbell. (Maureen and Bruce Herd)

Jimmy McDonald checking the champagne bottle is fixed properly prior to a launch,
with one of the joiners. (Maureen and Bruce Herd)

Jimmy Noble placing a gold
sovereign upon the keel of a vessel.
(Maureen and Bruce Herd)

Freedom, CN194.

A half model of *Ocean Reward* being
given to Skipper Saunderson's son by
Jimmy Noble at the launch celebrations.

Fred and Dorothy Normandale
with Jimmy Noble, at the launch
of *Independence*.

at a low interest rate for ten years, meaning he had to stump up a quarter. He agreed, and armed with a bridging loan from Barclays until he sold *Courage*, he rang Jimmy Noble and ordered the new boat. 'I paddled my own canoe,' he told me. 'Hence *Independence*, plus our first-born daughter Paula was born on July 4th.'

In his first book *First of the Flood* (Bottom End Publishing, 2002), Fred writes about the first time he visited Fraserburgh when, as a youngster, he had the chance of a trip aboard *Hazael* 3, FR107, one of Wilson Noble's boats. He'd sailed to North Shields and from there a coach took him and the crew back to Fraserburgh, where he'd been invited to stay the weekend along with his mate, Dennis. They'd chanced upon Jimmy Noble's yard when trekking around the harbour. Of it he wrote:

> Noble's yard was a hive of industry. We entered warily expecting to be ejected but were acknowledged with, 'hullo boys' or 'mornin' boys' by the workers we met. Inside the shed the oak skeleton of what seemed an immense ship was on the stocks. The air was full of the smell of sawdust and new wood, giving a warm pleasant sensation. Incessant hammering drew our eyes to a team of two shipwrights perched on a raised, trestle platform, each wielding a heavy hammer. Alternately they were belting a huge, square-shanked, galvanised nail into place in a four-inch-wide plank. Their timing was 'split second' and they never missed. A matching team worked a mirror image on the opposite side of the vessel. The ringing of their hammers echoed around the yard. Both pairs were in sight of each other through the ribs, but as the 'skin' grew on the bones, they'd become separated until the hull was intact.
>
> Later, slight gaps between the planks would be caulked with oakum, a rope-like substance, driven home … would swell amazingly when wet, making the vessel watertight. There were dozens of craftsmen working in harmony throughout the yard, giving life to this chrysalis. Horizontal sections of whole trees were being marked out and cut to the correct dimensions. These were planed by man and machine, then consigned to a 'steaming box', making them pliable. We were witnessing a creation and I was dumbstruck; my pal equally so.

In his second book he merely describes the corrugated iron building, 'like a giant hangar', which was the boatyard: 'The smell of new wood and fresh paint filled the air.' I note these as they are possibly the only written records of activity inside the yard from that era.

In 1980, like *Independence*, both *Piscean* and *Margaret Jane* (also for Scarborough) were transom-sterned, as was *Aspire*, LK239, built the same year. However, with orders thin on the ground and with the launch of the transom-sterned *Jasper 2*, PD174, completed, and Jimmy Noble facing retirement, the yard closed. I believe this was simply a financial decision, with the order book drying up and, if the company had strived to linger on, bankruptcy would probably have followed. Yankee had tried to persuade the others to diversify but these were uncertain times and both Jimmy and Charlie saw no future in this, and so the yard fell silent.

And so *Jasper 2* was the last new Fraserburgh-built vessel to be launched into the harbour and well over a hundred years of fishing boat building came to an abrupt end. Of course, Forbes continued battling on in Sandhaven, as well as repairing boats in Fraserburgh, while repairs were also undertaken by Buchan, Hall & Mitchell. But no new vessels were launched. Unfortunately, when Fred wanted a new boat in 1983, he had to go to J. & G. Forbes for *Emulator*, FR500, launched in February that year.

One question that gets asked fairly often is, 'What did they cost?' To understand this, we can look at three examples, one from 1932, another in 1949 and the last almost twenty years later, in 1968.

Florentine cost £850 complete in 1932. In 1949, Noble's quote for the 51ft *Liberty*, H580, was for a total of £5,443 6s 7d. The estimated hull cost was

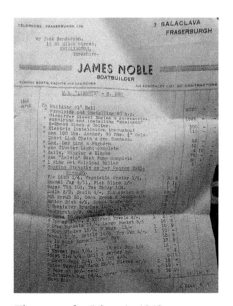

The quote for *Liberty* in 1949.

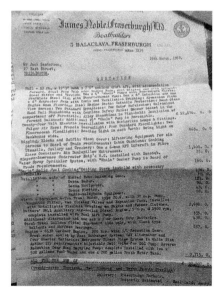

The quote for *Ocean Reward* in 1968.

£2,900 and the Gleniffer 80hp £1,925, with approximately £595 for fishing gear including a winch, along with over £23 for 'Cooking Utensils as per George Noble account'. This boat had been for Jack Sanderson of Bridlington.

In March 1968 Jack received another quote, and subsequently ordered *Ocean Reward*. The quote included the 52ft hull at £12,670, electrics £665, all internal gear etc. £1,100, trawl winch £2,690, trawl doors £657, generator £535, batteries £430, nav gear £510, marine toilet £75, water sprinkler system £160 and Gardner 200hp 8L3B £7,715, giving an overall total of £27,207.

While the cost for *Florentine* isn't broken down, it is for the other two. The largest increase percentage-wise of these was the hull from £2,690 to £12,670, a 4.71 times increase, while the engine cost also increased from £1,925 to £7,715 (a four times increase), although vast inroads had been made into engine construction, with the power rating rising from 80 to 200hp. Fishing gear, such as the drum winch and trawl doors, was not demanded aboard a seiner in 1949 but was commonplace aboard trawlers twenty years later, as modes of fishing changed. Furthermore, safety requirements demanded by the Board of Trade accounted for some increase in costs, as did other improvements such as 'reading lights over each berth'. One thing is always certain: costs increased year on year in almost everything – it's called inflation! Compare these to the price of £3,000 Wilson Noble received for the 69ft *Dundarg* in 1939.

Turntable ferry *Appin Chief*. (Maureen and Bruce Herd)

Nevertheless, by the time Noble's had launched *Jasper 2* down the ways in 1981, costs had rocketed once again for those companies left in the industry. We have already seen how Fred Normandale had to stump up £160,000 for *Independence* in 1980. Other yards, such as Forbes, a few miles along the coast, and Macduff, many more miles in the same direction, continued to work. Forbes' fared for another twenty years, although by the time it finally closed up its large shed doors, wooden boatbuilding within the fishing industry had all but passed into obscurity. Macduff and C. Toms in Polruan, Cornwall, both persevered with a handful of new builds for a few more years, but generally wood was seen as inferior to all the advantages of steel – strength, cost and ease of construction. Macduff's built its last wooden boat in 2004, this being the 11.95m *Iris*, BRD19. Luke Powell and others' aspiration that they can match the price for wood against steel for under 10m vessels remains to be put into practice, especially given world market upheavals in steel production. I hope it happens but, at the same time, I'll admit I'm not holding my breath. Fingers crossed, hey!

WORKING IN THE YARD

Given the time lapse, it was difficult to find people who worked in the yard, although I was lucky to find Bobby Jones who, at the age of 89, was able to say that he was the only person remaining who worked in all five yards at Fraserburgh – Wilson Noble, Tommy Summers, Jimmy Noble, Buchan, Hall & Mitchell and, very briefly, at Forbes. Because he worked for both Wilson and Jimmy, some of Bobby's story is told in a subsequent chapter.

Willie McRobbie started work some months before he began his apprenticeship in March 1970 and went on to serve the full six years before leaving. He remembers how working there was hard, and cold in the winter with the wind whistling in through all the gaps in the shed. Yet, he says, there was always a good working atmosphere. His first wage was £5 at the end of that first week in 1969.

Just as an apprentice should, he says he learnt all aspects of the job, from cutting out frames from slabs of oak at the bandsaw, to setting up the frames, fairing the hull, planking, caulking, spar-making and some finishing work. Yankee McDonald was in charge of the finishing work, which took place either in the finishing sheds along the back wall of the yard or upon the boat alongside the quay after the launch. Bobby described him as a quiet person: 'Oh, yes, he was really good at his work.' All three directors worked in the yard while, on official occasions such as launches, they were suitably dressed in suits to impress the clientele.

Charlie Noble was the foreman and supervisor, and even though folk knew he had a bit of a drink problem, they say it didn't interfere with his work. One person described him as 'harmless'. But he was always on hand and Robbie described one day how he was working a two-man crosscut saw, sitting on some fish boxes as he worked. Charlie came along and kicked the boxes away, telling him to either stand or kneel at the job. There'd be no sitting around on the job, he told him in no uncertain terms. And, like Jimmy junior, he was called 'the ghost' as both of them had the knack of managing to appear out of the blue when the men were working. They said that you'd be working when one of them would suddenly be almost breathing down your neck. Perhaps the mark of good management!

Of Jimmy himself, I asked Willie McRobbie whether he was 'fearsome'. 'No,' he replied, 'but he was firm.' Bobby Jones described him as a 'grumpy old bugger'! Another respondent laughed when I mentioned this, describing him as 'dour'. 'He'd no sense of humour,' they added. Another skipper, Graeme Jack, who commissioned *Moray Lass*, INS104 (1952), and *Faithful*, INS38 (1970), described James senior as 'one of the finest men along the coast'. What was clear was that, however they all were, they gained the respect of everybody that they came across: fishermen and workforce. Theirs was a reputation that lingered and is still talked about. Noble by name and nature, thus.

Like any business, there was a small office alongside the main shed. Jimmy's secretary was, for many years, Bessie Campbell, who retired only a few years before the yard closed and has since died. She has been described as the admin brains behind the company. Nan Williamson took over for a very short period and today she remembers the *Margaret Jane* being launched for the Mainprizes and another for Shetland, which presumably was *Aspire*. Nothing much else, she apologised. 'They've all gone,' she said, dishearteningly.

Charlie Noble, the son of Charlie as already mentioned, who worked in the yard for nine months in 1960, told me his first job of the day was to light the fire in the office to keep Bessie and Jimmy warm. One can only imagine the copious amounts of paperwork that must have been inside that room, which, when the yard closed in 1981, was consigned to a skip. Records, drawings, specifications, quotes: all got rid of. Charlie clearly remembers the *Wavesheaf*, INS118, being launched. He also threw some light on the ferry building as he told me that several were either planned or built while he was there. Combine these with several yachts and we see a clear picture that, although fishing boats were the main concern, James Noble's original plan to branch out had, to a very limited extent, been a reality. Yet, compared with some of the other Scottish builders – Forbes, Millers or Herd & Mackenzie, for instance – Noble's output of a handful of yachts was small fry. Nevertheless, over almost half a century the yard persevered and ended a proud and noble tradition begun by Alexander Noble more than eighty years before. Given the nature of fishing boats today, surely that's something to write home about!

2

THE LAUNCH OF A NOBLE'S BOAT

The launch of any new boat is a celebration for those involved in its construction and future ownership. For a fishing boat, which is often a family investment in terms of both finance and knowledge, it is a cause to involve those around them, not just their immediate family, but friends from within, and without, the fishing industry.

But, in days gone past, it would have attracted a good audience of locals, especially in Fraserburgh, where much of local employment figured around the harbour. If you weren't a member of the fishing industry, you would probably be involved in some ancillary way: boatbuilding, upkeep and repair; engineering and fabrication; painting; ships' chandlery and fishing gear; victualling of vessels or some other parallel works. Seldom would a launch be without a good crowd of onlookers to cheer as the boat hit the water. And it didn't only attract people from these trades: school children would be mesmerised by such occasions.

Very often a launch was a very formal affair, and could, because of the scarcity of boatbuilders around the coasts, involve wrangling the logistics of getting family and friends to the boatyard from their bases miles away. The availability and cost of hotel accommodation could, in these cases, be foremost in deciding whom to invite.

Generally, if people had travelled from afar, the first gathering of the day would be to inspect the vessel in the yard, before heading off to get ready for the main event. Thus folk would assemble again at the yard in their Sunday best, the family taking their pride of place at the bow, where a swinging pendulum fixed to the stem would have been positioned, with the traditional bottle of champagne clamped in its jaws, ready and waiting to be smashed against the stem immediately prior to launch. The yard workers would also be present, some making last-minute adjustments to ensure the boat slid into the water smoothly and without hitch. Once the boat was launched, they would probably be rewarded with a bottle or two of beer.

We will look at the technical sides of these launches from both yards.

WILSON NOBLE

To start with, Wilson Noble had no slip and had to launch off the quayside directly into the harbour. The photos here show vessels in the years just prior to the Second World War (1937, 1938 and 1939).

A hazy *Mayflower* prior to launch, 1937. (Maureen Small)

Harmony, FR 416, about to be towed out of the shed, 1938.

The photo of *Mayflower* ready for launch shows what looks like a section of the quayside in front of the shed with slightly angled edges (shown within the darker stones) and probably about 18ft in width. When the minesweeper MMS10 was launched in 1939 as the first of many, she was launched off the wall upon a timber structure which was cut into the quayside. Presumably this technique was improved upon as the war progressed, especially in 1943 when the larger 140ft minesweepers were being launched.

BANQUET
TO COMMEMORATE THE LAUNCH OF
"M.M.S. 10"
FROM THE BOATBUILDING YARD OF
MESSRS. WILSON NOBLE & CO., BALACLAVA
THURSDAY, 31st OCTOBER AT 1 P.M.   LAUNCH BY MRS W. NOBLE

The official launch of MMS10 in 1939. (Maureen Small)

The official toast list for the launch. Rachael Wilson performed the ceremony. (Maureen Small)

TOAST LIST

THE KING
Provost Thompson, Chairman

THE ROYAL NAVY
Hon. Sheriff Substitute J. D. McIntosh
Reply: Commander Coppinger, R.N.

PRESENTATION OF MEMENTO TO MRS NOBLE
Bailie John Dunbar, J.P.

THE BUILDERS
Bailie John Dunbar, J.P.   Reply: Mr Wilson Noble

TOWN AND TRADE OF FRASERBURGH
Mr William Malcolm   Reply: Provost J. M. Thompson

VOTE OF THANKS TO CHAIRMAN
Captain A. Stephen

When we then consider the launchings of *Xmas Star* (1955) and *True Vine* (1957), we can see how the vessels are running upon timber ways. In the photo of *True Vine*, the cutaway in the quayside is clearly visible. The photograph of *Flourish*, FR149, launched by Tommy Summers after he briefly took over the yard after Wilson closed, also clearly shows the ways through the same cut-out in the quayside (see page 55).

Bobby Jones recalls that the yard had permission to prevent vehicles travelling along the quayside for three days prior to a launch while the workforce prepared by removing the stone and building the ways. They then had a day following the launch to clear away the timber and fill in the quay before traffic was allowed along again.

Xmas Star, FR87, at launch.

True Vine after launch.

JAMES NOBLE

James Noble had a slipway in front of his main shed that made life easier, although the slip did not belong to the yard so temporary measures had to be be adopted and permission obtained. The slip was also used by Tommy Summers, who pulled his smaller vessels along the breakwater and launched vessels down on timber rollers. For his larger vessels, James Noble was able to build ways directly from his shed. The smaller vessels built in the small shed that was next to the Northern Engineering Co. shed would be dragged out and launched directly over the quay, sometimes sideways, as in the cases of *Fiona Fay* and *Castle Eden*, both 49ft and launched in 1958. From photographs it is clear that both were launched directly off the quay to one side of the slipway. Unfortunately for the 72ft *Fertility*, launched in 1953, the photo doesn't show how she got into the water!

However, for the others, *Procyon* (1956), *Maureen* (1963), *Enchanter* (1967), *Ocean Reward* (1969) and *Devotion* (1978), temporary ways had been built as shown in the various photographs.

The work of constructing the ways for the launch would have been carried out on the days leading up to the event. A solid framework was constructed: huge blocks of wood of a corresponding height laid out with a hefty piece atop each side as the runners. Support in the form of struts gave the ways their lateral strength. The photo of the ways during the launch of *Iris*, FR7, in 1968, clearly illustrates how they were constructed and how copious amounts of soft soap were applied to the top of each runner (seen being applied in the photo of the stern view of *Enchanter*) or the ways, so that the vessel, supported by the blocks, ran down when the launch was to begin. High tide was obviously the time for this.

The hull itself was lowered onto a sort of steel trolley that ran on the timber, chocked up with vertical lumps of wood following the shape of the belly of the hull over the midship section, as the photo of the stern of *Ocean Reward* shows. This was all held together with steel wire passing below the keel. This fell away into the harbour once the boat was afloat, and it was later reclaimed from the water and brought ashore. The launching preparation would take the whole workforce at least three days to complete.

Of course, the launch would attract a crowd of locals, and the friends and workmates of the owners would no doubt be invited. Crawford Rosie admitted to skiving off school for such an event! Those with official invitations would all gather for the ceremony, at which time either Jimmy Noble or Yankee McDonald would probably introduce the family and then the person chosen to launch the vessel – often the wife or daughter of the fisherman – would bless 'the vessel and all that sail in her'. They would then swing the bottle of champagne at the bow, and hopefully smash it at the first throw, although the photograph of the small 32ft *Kindly Light* shows the launch upon the slipway with the bottle being smashed by hand against the stem! The photo of *Betty* clearly shows the swinging pendulum bottle holder fixed to the stem.

Maureen Herd, Yankee's daughter, remembers giving watches or jewellery to some of the wives of the skippers in the later days of the yard. 'It was normally a watch,' she told me.

The aforementioned photo of *Iris* about to slide down the ways also shows how today's somewhat over-the-top health and safety regulations didn't apply back then, with a good crowd gathered all around the ways. Today there would be 6ft-high Heras fencing erected, if such a launch was even allowed!

Once so christened, the boat would then begin to glide down the slippery ways, once the men had knocked out the last supporting wedge, and into the water at high tide. It would then be moored alongside the quayside for the guests to climb aboard. Celebrations would continue with a grand meal at the Alexandra Hotel, and perhaps a party atmosphere with dancing that went on long into the night. For the workforce, bottles of beer were sent down for them to drink before the deconstruction of the ways would begin. Each launch was a big affair and a financial drag on the business as the yard paid for all the accommodation and for the celebratory party, drinks included. And if Jimmy and Charlie's partaking was anything to go by, that could amount to a jolly big bill!

The Tommy Summers-built *Flourish* showing the built-up slipway.

Fertility, PD267, showing how light she is in the water after launching. Ballast, engine and gear, winch and fitting out will take her to the contact waterline.

The launch of *Incentive*, PD349. She got stuck halfway down the slip and had to be pulled by a lorry from across the harbour.

Procyon, INS7, sliding down the ways, watched by a good crowd.

Older-style ferry being launched.

One of the turntable-type ferries
on launch.(Maureen and Bruce Herd)

Maureen, WK270, producing an
impressive wave on her launch.

The start of the launch of
Enchanter, FR 408.

Enchanter as she hits the water.

Ocean Reward, FR 28, as she slides into
the harbour.

Preparing for the launch of *Ocean Reward*. Jimmy Noble is on the starboard side and
Bobby Jones (with lighter top) on the port side spreading the soft soap onto the ways.

Ocean Reward, being launched
without her wheelhouse,
enters the water.

Stern view of *Enchanter* as the
ways are being smothered in
soft soap.

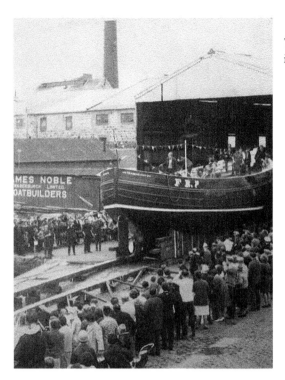

The launch of *Iris*, FR7, in 1975.

The smaller *Kindly Light* being launched, already upon the quay.

The bottle smashes against the stem of *Betty*, FR 68, already in the water.

The launch of the motor yacht *Lynette*, undated. (Maureen and Bruce Herd)

An unnamed Noble yacht, similar to *Sheemaun*. (Maureen and Bruce Herd)

Jimmy McDonald presenting a keepsake of the launch of *Margaret Jane* to
Mrs Maggie Mainprize, along with the other two directors, Jimmy Noble junior
and Charlie Noble junior, who took over the running of the yard after Jimmy
senior died. (Maureen and Bruce Herd)

Assembled company celebrating the launch of *Margaret Jane*.
(Maureen and Bruce Herd)

The administrative brains behind
the company, Mrs Bessie Campbell
(née Webster), being presented
with a floral tribute after a launch.
(Maureen and Bruce Herd)

L–R: Mrs Bessie Campbell, Miss Maureen McDonald, Mrs Jimmy McDonald and Mrs Jessie Noble. (Maureen and Bruce Herd)

The launch of the *Enchanter* in 1967 shows just how popular any launch would be.

3

MEMORIES

Rather than simply recounting endless boat names and the way developments changed the face of fishing and affected both Noble yards, I concluded that it would be better to listen to those who knew the yards, or the boats, and spent some – or all – of their working lives building or working such vessels. Thanks to contacts in and around Fraserburgh, and helped by family members, I've been able to speak to several people who have given me stories of some relevance to both Wilson and James Noble.

BOBBY JONES AND THE STING THAT HAD GONE BUT CAUSED ALARM

I left school at 14 and worked in a hairdressers until I was 16. I started serving my time in 1948 at Wilson Noble's, the only yard at that time. An apprenticeship was for five years, standard procedure at that time.

When we were bairns, in the 1930s, before the Second World War broke out, I was Robert John Ritchie, but there were two or three Robert John Ritchies and I became known as Robert John, then Bobby John and then it became Bobby Jones. There are people who have gone to their grave in Fraserburgh not knowing I was Bobby Ritchie, thinking I was Bobby Jones.

Between the two wars Old Wilson had four sons: Wilson, Alexander, James and Charlie. There must have been a falling out or something afore the war as two (James and Charlie) decided to take a walk and set up James Noble Company. But Charlie never had a share in the firm. As I said, I started serving my time in 1948. I was there to 1953 until my time was out. Then I was away to the army, National Service, for two years. I came out and was back at Wilson's because at that time there was a law that said the firm you were with before National Service had to give you a year's work after. So then I was there for a year and then out, unemployed for two weeks, I was single and didn't give a damn. Then I was walking along to Tommy Summers' yard and asked if there was any chance of a job. 'Aye, OK,' he said.

So I was meant to be there on a short-term basis but I was there for eight years. That was when Tommy finished. Then I worked for Brook Marine for nine weeks, down Lowestoft. When I came back I started at Jimmy's. So I was with the three firms, though I was with the fourth with Johnny Wilson but they were never building, just repairs. I finished my last fifteen years' employment 'til my retirement with them, Buchan, Hall & Mitchell, though I did work for a few months at Forbes in between. Because by that time the last boat built in Fraserburgh had been launched. The last boat launched into the harbour from Jimmy Noble's was the *Jasper* (*Jasper 2*, PD174, 59.3ft, built for G. Forman, Peterhead).

When Tommy started up, Wilson's gradually petered out. The yard lay empty for a wee while, then Tommy took it into his business but he had boats building at the breakwater so he split the squad up. Some went down to work at Wilson's and some, including myself, stayed at the breakwater. But when those boats were done at the breakwater the whole squad finished up at Wilson's.

When Tommy started up, there was Bill Duthie and George McLeman. They were working in Jimmy's and decided to set up. There must have been orders as you wouldn't do a thing like that and sit and twiddle your thumbs waiting for a boat. There must have been definite orders.

Most of the big wood, slabs, and that for frames, keels and all like that came from Hull. Brought up by Fleming's lorries. At the start there was no formica, it was all lining boards, tongue and groove and that. The joiners were responsible for the cabins and the wheelhouses but all that came before it (the hull, deck and all) was the carpenters. Deck work. Never specialised in one thing. As far as the outside work was, the steelwork was provided by Mitchells. The electrical work was R. Dean Downie, and the engineering, John Pirie. The jobs changed as the years went by. As to the tools and that, the hand tools we had needed two hands. It was like a prehistoric age with the tools we used to now. No chainsaws then. Only big lumps, a cross cut, a man in each channel, slow, slow work. It was all done manually.

Getting the frames up was a squad job. Frames went up, one by one, manually. Tommy's at the yard had a crane but at the breakwater it was all manually. For the bigger boats with double frames, it was twice the weight and twice the time to cut the frames. You'd got to cut each frame twice. Even though they were double they had a slightly different shape. You'd get the shape from the moulds, using pencil or chalk. Pencil gave a more accurate line.

Mostly it was fishing boats, at Wilson's it was all fishing boats. At Jimmy's, he specialised after the war when I first came to it, was ring-netters. Varnished ring-netters, that was his speciality. Not a ring-netter at Wilson's and Tommy never built any either. Varnished boats with silver-painted gunwales. Bonny boats, about 50-odd feet.

At Wilson's there were minesweepers, mine layers, all the big yards were building during the war, all under the government. And in Jimmy's I think.

Jimmy Noble was married but had no family. There was Charlie, he had a Jimmy Noble, so this Jimmy, Jimmy senior's nephew, took over the business. There seemed to be a bit of animosity between Charlie and Jimmy's wife. So when Jimmy retired, wife Jess Hendry took control and when Jimmy died (he didn't last long after he retired) she had the whole controlling interest. I think that she maybe had a sister who married a McDonald, which would have made Yankee a nephew. When she died she left the whole caboodle to him, so he had the controlling interest.

I knew him when he was younger and he played football for the Broch, and I never ever heard him speak any American. He took full control, he was a joiner by trade, but the firm was run by Charlie and his two sons, Jimmy and Charlie. Charlie worked with his hands. When Charlie died, they got a share in the firm but their father Charlie never had a share in the firm.

Wilson's were 70–75ft fishing boats, his speciality. Jimmy was into the ring-netters, 50–60ft. Forbes at Sandhaven built big boats, too.

How long to build a boat, depends on its size. At Jimmy's from the day the keel was laid to the day the boat was launched was seven weeks but that was when we going fast on bonus. But when a boat was launched it was only half done. It needed fitting out, engine, tanks, wheelhouse. It was all fitted out in the harbour until it was finished.

When it came to launching, at Wilson Noble's they were launched straight into the water, there was a slip there, but the last part was filled in so that the traffic could pass along the harbour. But for three days before a launch and one day after a launch, we were allowed to lift it and break up the road so that traffic couldnae pass in front of the yard. Jimmy launched into that small slip in front of the yard.

Tommy launched straight off the breakwater, straight off the pier. Then he got an order for two very large boats, the *WFP* and *Ada Kirby*, for Lowestoft so he had to build a slip. And after they were launched, they were still building smaller boats, and he'd built a big slip and they launched down the slip. Yawls were dragged on their keels to Jimmy Noble's slip and launched. Fuel lorries, they would tow the boats with a big wire around a block.

In 1972 Jimmy launched the *Edelweiss*, FR014, with a forward engine, and after Jimmy said he'd never launch a boat with a forward engine again. Five frames cracked, and insurance claim.

I was with another fellow under the *Lilacina* when she was launched from Tommy's prematurely when someone waved and the lorry driver took it as a signal. The boats were sitting on massive logs, bolted down, and I was under it with another man with a sorting out a jack and suddenly the keel started moving. I looked at him and he looked at me and we got out and I was shaking for half an hour. I saw Tommy afterwards and shouted, 'Good launch that, good launch, you nearly killed us!'

During the war, I was not there, was still at school, but during the war they were building minesweepers, minelayers, and they had platforms on them, built to strengthen them to contain depth charges. The depth charges were drums and they had to be the exact weight.

So that after the war, when I started serving my time, I started in 1948, so this was about 1949, 1950, maybe. We were clearing out a corner of the yard, and there were these so-called depth charges, been lying there for ages. So we had instructions, me and Willie Doran, take one and spoil it. With a great struggle we got it on a barrow. We were taking it around to the cove, round the side of Maconochie's factory, round the back of Jimmy's Lowe's yard. But on the way there we met two carpenters coming from the pontoon and one was carrying a tin of paint, and asked me if I'd take a tin back to the yard. Fair enough. So we took the tin of paint, Willie Doran, my partner, and me got the barrow on top of the brae and rolled it off, and being a heavy thing it bounced, bounced, bounced right down to the water, into the water. It lay in the water, it didnae sink, even though it was heavy. So I came back up, and as I was standing looking down, the devil got into me. I says to Willie, 'Give me that tin of paint and a brush.' I went down and painted a swastika on the side of the depth charge, and *Achtung*. Attention! And away we went, quite happily.

About a week after, there was a policeman down to the yard, how about this? They'd just discovered it, been lying there a week. They discovered it and a big fuss got up. The policeman, been guarding it night and day, twenty-four hours a day, been up on top of the brae, and they phoned and got a bomb disposal team up from Rosyth. But they got as far as Aberdeen and they stopped them when they discovered what had actually happened. But to be on the safe side they evacuated the factory, all the women were evacuated. Jimmy

Garden went down with a cold chisel and a hammer and bust it open. But the police didnae come down then, stayed up on top of the brae. That was an infamous incident. It was splattered all over the papers. All over the papers and the headline in the evening paper said 'Blessed my heart – its sting had gone but it caused alarm'. I went home to my granny's and she was sat reading the paper and laughing. She wouldn't have been laughing if she'd found out it was me that did it.

Anyway, me and my partner in crime were summoned to appear in the Fraserburgh court. And we went up to the court in the morning and the police sergeant was standing at the door collecting the summons and as we handed ours he says, 'You the two buggers who tried to blow up the Broch.' The funny side's past but then comes the serious side. We were fined a week's wages, which was a lot of money in those days. But if it hadn't been for that tin of paint and brush, it would never have happened. I'd have never thought of it!

Young Wilson was a hard man, he'd chase me round the yard with big thick boots to clip my ears. There was this great big vat of boiling pitch when they were pitching the decks and the like, the bottoms of the boats. He came along, it was summer, shirt sleeves right up past the elbows, and he slipped and his hand went right into the boiling pitch. Christ, sweat came out on his face, but he never gave a swalk. A hard man, him, and I liked him. Old Wilson was good at Burns suppers, great thing with the Tam O'Shanter and that. But Young Wilson was not good with poems and that.

THE STORM OF '53: THE LIFEBOAT LOSS AND BEACH 13

The storm of January 1953 is well etched into the memories of those who experienced the horrific winds that reached 100mph in parts of the country. The North Sea was funnelled under such a wind strength that, with 39ft waves lashing the coast, destruction was widespread. In the Netherlands, 1,400 people lost their lives, while hundreds were drowned along the eastern side of England. A ferry sank in the Irish Sea with hundreds aboard.

One onlooker recalled:

I remember that storm, even though I was only 5 years old in Peterhead. The screaming of the wind scared me. The green lino in my bedroom rising and falling. My parents holding me up at the window overlooking South Bay. The corrugated roof from the neighbour's shed taking off across the embankment. The villages of Gamrie and Crovie took a hammering, with houses demolished, and villagers moved out of their homes, which were washed out by sea, never to return to them.

It had been Burns Night and some folk came out of their village halls at one o'clock in the morning and instantly felt the power of the storm. 'Never heard anything like it before then, and since ...,' Gladys Mackenzie told reporters. In Fraserburgh, Wilson Noble, at the ripe old age of 72, was presumably at the Burns Night supper, though probably not addressing the haggis that year!

Also in Fraserburgh, the lifeboat *John and Charles Kennedy* went out to escort some small yawls back into harbour and as she returned she was hit herself by a huge wave that capsized her, with only one crew member surviving.

Over on the west coast, at Ullapool, the crews came back on the morning of 31 January after a weekend at home to find that their vessels had been washed onto the beaches. For Ullapool this wasn't anything new: some fifty years before, the sailing fishing fleet there had been driven ashore by a January gale.

But this one was different. The boats were bigger and they lay in different spots around Loch Broom. Some were beached at Corry Point – *Snowflake*, PD812, the last big boat built at Gamrie, and *Boy David*, BF309 – where they were banged up against each other. They were the easiest to relaunch. Thirteen ended up at Ardcharnich Bay, by Rubh an Olan, and this later became known as Beach 13! One was at Inverlael and was dragged back into the sea with a bulldozer.

The fisherman's mission was too small and so tents were set up and fishermen taken into the church and village halls; even the Women's Guild and the whist club helped out. The whole town rallied round, for most were from the east coast. Soup kitchens were set up to feed the hungry workers; the fishermen and carpenters, locals and army. Navy personnel from Aultbea arrived after a couple of days; remember that the roads were little more than single track. The specialist salvage vessel HMS *Barneath* was brought in, too.

Royal Engineers from Elgin arrived to help refloat all the vessels, many of which had a connection to Fraserburgh such as the 1-year-old Tommy Summers-built *Morning Star*, PD234. She ended up on Beach 13, where she nearly suffered a complete disaster as she was being pulled towards the sea and a chock shifted. Ironically, I suppose, she survived, only to be wrecked in the Sound of Mull twenty years later.

Some of the other boats were: *Margaret Reid*, LK440; the Forbes-built *Gowan Lea*, FR130; and *Crimond*, BCK187.

The process of refloating the vessels was complex. First the wooden hulls were high and dry, well above the height of the high tide. The rudders and propellers were dug out and the shingle moved either by hand or with Charlie Tait's bulldozer so that a cradle could be constructed and the hulls repaired by carpenters, who were brought in from the boatyards on the Broch.

As Bobby Jones recalls:

It was my last year apprenticing at Wilson Noble's. The lifeboat washed up the back of the breakwater, upside down, she was, on the rocks. At the time there'd been severe gales and a lot of the fishing boats fishing on the west coast were washed ashore at Ullapool. So the carpenters were all over there to get the boats off and it was down to the apprentices left in the Broch. So Wilson's apprentices and Jimmy's apprentices had the job of getting the boat off the rocks and round onto the slip to get dismantled. Well, it was a big job, but we managed it when the seas died down. The day for getting her off, I remember, six o'clock in the morning they had us down there. Towed round by the pilot, upside down and onto the slip. Within three days there was nothing left. RNLI came to collect the engines and buoyancy tanks and the rest went to Wilson's scrapyard. Buoyancy tanks lay alongside Wilson's for many years.

In Ullapool, for each vessel, a makeshift slipway had to be dug down to the sea below and once these stages were complete, the boat was refloated, helped by the lifting gear of the *Barneath*, to ensure a smooth entry into the loch. Sometimes this refloating process had to be repeated, and once one boat was afloat, then they'd move on to the next. One photograph shows all the thirteen boats on Ardcharnich Bay still beached two weeks after the storm, showing just how long the whole process took. *Crimond* was the last vessel to be refloated. She then went away to Scalloway, to Moores boatyard, and had a 114hp Gardner engine put in.

GEORGE FORBES AND THE 'BASTARD MAHOGANY'

George Forbes was apprenticed to James Noble & Co. at the age of 15, one of six apprentices at the time. His father, Charles, was working in the yard, as had his grandfather, who worked there for thirty-three years in total. George talks about his early days and how he managed to gather a good collection of tools. Just a few months before he started there his great uncle died and so his father was able to negotiate with his great aunt to purchase these tools. Once he started work, Jimmy Noble produced what tools he didn't have but needed and George paid for these through minimum deductions from his weekly pay packet. His tool box was made in the joinery shop, which was the building between the main shed and the smaller shed, where he recalls there were four permanent joiners.

In his set were two adzes, both slightly different. He mentioned that no one in the yard had the same adze as they all suited the individual owner, the same as the handle. Then there were his brace and bits, big boring drills, hammer, caulking mallet and irons, planes, saw, flat scraper and rasp – all capable of being neatly housed in the box. When, after the war, many carpenters had to go to Grangemouth in search of work when boatbuilding was scarce, they needed a minimum of luggage.

He also notes that his father would have been in charge over Tommy Summers and Bill Duthie during the time of their apprenticeships. Other than the apprentices, photos show a workforce of twenty-eight, including Jimmy Noble (boss), James Noble (boss's son), Charlie Noble (boss's father) and James McDonald (joiner and co-owner). Other than them, it was a mixture of apprentices, labourers, joiners and carpenters.

George's photos of hulls being built show the staging precariously balanced on tall trestles, set-ups that today would give any health and safety executive a heart attack. Frames, made up from the moulds, and cut on a bandsaw, were hauled up by hand. One photo shows the topsides being added to the frames, the wood being oak for the first four or five planks down so that wear was a minimum when boats were moored alongside each other. The lower planks were larch. The deck was described as a 'bastard mahogany, hard wearing'.

STRATHYRE, INS23

Wrecked at Lossiemouth Harbour, February 1958
A siren was warning boats of the danger
John Heron, *The Northern Scot, 15 February 1958*

Mountainous seas and heavy swell caused chaotic conditions in Lossiemouth harbour on Sunday morning where one vessel was wrecked and several others damaged.

The luckless vessel was the *Strathyre*, INS 23, launched only 11 months ago [at Noble's of Fraserburgh] at the cost of some £16,000. Her skipper, 34-year-old Mr Alec Souter (Jasper) of 12 Coulardhill, last year won the Boyd Anderson Trophy for the top aggregate catch landed at the port (for vessels of 50 feet or over).

First hint of the conditions in the harbour came at 7 a.m. when Mr Charles Milne (30) of the Brander Arms looked out of his bedroom window. 'It was very dark,' he said, 'but I noticed the masts of a vessel where no mast ought to be. I threw on some clothes and ran to the police station.' The harbour master was roused and the siren which warns crews when something is amiss at the harbour was set off. The *Strathyre* was found to have broken her moorings and drifted across the channel to the spending beach, 'the graveyard of the *Briar Rose* less than a year before'. One of the latest additions to the fleet, the *Olive Leaf*, had also broken adrift and she and some other vessels all berthed in East Basin were considerably damaged. Hurriedly crews ran out extra ropes.

When daylight broke it was seen that the *Strathyre*'s rudder had been torn away and her keel smashed. With a big tide due at high water (just after 3 p.m.) it was thought that the stricken *Strathyre* might be re-floated. Skippers James Souter of the *Atlantas* and Alec Flett of the *Arcadia* took their vessels into the entrance of the East Basin. Held between the quayside by heavy ropes and buffeted about by the swell, the vessels passed two ropes to the

The wrecking of the *Strathyre*, INS23, at Lossiemouth in 1958.

Strathyre in an attempt to pull her off by winch. A further nylon line was passed to her from a crane.

Willing helpers on the shore lent a hand in the fight to save the *Strathyre* by manhandling block and tackle in an effort to pull the vessel's bow round into the channel (she had been driven ashore broadside on). For a time it looked that they might succeed. For some four hours the struggle went on, but the sea won. Gradually the *Strathyre* was driven solidly on the boulders and the crashing waves stove in her timbers. She had to be written off.

In all some 35 vessels were berthed in the East Basin and few of them escaped undamaged. Damage varying from minor scrapes to havoc estimated to cost many pounds was caused. A lobster boat belonging to Mr Bob Stewart of MacDonald Drive was completely wrecked at the same spot as the *Strathyre*. On Monday the task of salvaging the *Strathyre*'s valuable gear fishing aids and her engine commenced.

Yarning - A Few Facebook Quotes on *Evangeline*

Davie Watt:

My grandad Laurence Buchan had the *Evangeline*, FR163. He bought her from Tarbert [in 1947] where he fished a lot in his earlier years; working the sma-lines out of the Broch in the winter. I spent my early teens aboard her all summer out at the mackerel and in the winter I redded up sma-lines after school & my mam would bait them with mussels she had spent all morning de-shelling into enamel pails ... stinking, blooming things (still can't eat mussels to this day) but I can still smell them. The *Evangeline* & *Vesper* were partners at the sprat fishing up at Inverness.

Brian Walker:

The *Evangeline* used to come up to Burghead to the prawns, early '60s.

Bob Anderson:

Vesper worked out of Burghead in the mid-70s.

Robert Cowe:

Went to the great-lines and the sprats at Inverness on the *Evangeline* with James Buchan, who lost his life in the Fraserburgh lifeboat disaster in 1970. The last time I saw her was in Tayport. I remember catching a barn door skate, which covered the deck. At one time the *Vesper* was owned by Alex Ross, who worked the hand-lines.

I remember being at the pair trawling at Inverness when both boats came together, one rope holding the two, and the work was done on one boat by both crews. It being choppy, the boats separated and the *Evangeline* took off on her own. Thankfully most of the catch was on board so we had to chase the unmanned *Evangeline* to get crew onto her! On another occasion we caught the undercarriage of an airplane.

Mike Smylie (Author):

I remember Brian Watson, the harbourmaster at Pittenweem in 2001, owned her until she caught fire at Anstruther. She was a complete burn-out.

Evangeline.

4

SOME SURVIVORS

WILSON NOBLE: THE *VIOLET*/*VESPER* STORY

Violet was built for Alexander Grieve Stephen and cost about £190. She was named after his youngest daughter, who had been born the previous year. She fished at the lines, while following the local herring during the season. At first she worked under sail but, as her launch coincided with the early installations of engines into fishing boats, she was soon engined with a 13.15hp Kelvin sleeve valve, later replaced with a 30hp Kelvin and, in 1936, a 48hp Gardner. She continued to work right up to 1975 and was renowned for being in tip-top condition. She was then sold and eventually ended up in Martha's Vineyard, where she was restored by Gary Maynard. He, with his wife, sailed her widely until she was sold in Chicago in 2013 where, presumably, she still is.

Vesper, on the other hand, was built for George Noble and John Buchan and we can only wonder whether this is the same George Noble who pops up as a partner in Wilson Noble & Co. until resigning in 1939. Whether he was a cousin or even more distant relative is unknown. With Noble being a common surname in Fraserburgh, it is possible that there was no connection other than a business one.

In 1935 *Vesper* was sold to Alexander Duthie Stephen, brother of Alexander Grieve, who had been skippering her for a number of years. There was a report in the local Fraserburgh paper about his great seamanship in the face of one of the worst north-easterly gales seen in the Moray Firth. Working at the lines, all was hauled before Skipper Stephen, with crew John Watt and his son George Watt, made for Fraserburgh but they were unable to enter the harbour with the wind having increased. Thus they decided to head into the Moray Firth, around Kinnaird Head, and try to shelter there. It appears her progress was being watched closely by a crowd onshore and the Fraserburgh lifeboat was

Violet alongside the small yawl *Fragrance*.

Violet being transported from the streets of Massachusetts, USA.

sent out. This was later replaced by the Whitehills lifeboat and *Vesper* then made for Gardenstown, only to be warned off by a signal flag showing 'danger'. They proceeded westwards to Macduff where, followed by the lifeboat astern, they made for the harbour. The newspaper reported: 'To the horror of those watching on shore, the *Vesper* made as if to come straight in to the spending beach instead of making for the harbour mouth', although Skipper Stephen obviously realised his mistake and turned about, being 'overtaken' by huge waves that 'seemed to swallow her up, but she gamely reappeared'. She came straight in again, but, almost in, she was struck by a huge wave and 'the shout went up from hundreds of throats, "She's on the rocks."' But she wasn't and 'with a Herculean wrench at the wheel' Stephen brought her bows round towards the harbour, missed the rocks and shot into the harbour, only missing the pier on the other side with another desperate turn of the wheel. Obviously the crowd, and the reporter, were extremely impressed with Skipper Stephen's seamanship.

She worked from various ports over time and changed hands several times before landing up at Buckie in the early 1990s, where she was then put ashore, looking very sad in her dilapidated state. The owner at the time had great ideas about forming an association and was looking for grants to restore her, but nothing came of it and she was eventually broken up in the early 2000s.

Vesper.

WILSON NOBLE: DUNDARG, FR121

The 69ft herring drifter *Dundarg* was launched into the Balaclava harbour in 1939, the twelfth boat launched from Fraserburgh yards that year. At the time, the yard did not have a slipway, so she was pushed/dragged off the quay wall at high water. She was built to order for James Duthie and others from Rosehearty, and cost some £3,000. Mrs Duthie, wife of the skipper, named her at the launch ceremony on 17 August.

She is named after the ruined castle of that name just outside of Fraserburgh. The Gaelic '*Dundarg*' roughly translates to 'Red Fort': '*Dun*' being 'Fort' and '*Dearg*' being 'Red'. It is for this reason that various owners have kept the boat painted a red colour.

The boat made one successful fishing trip to East Anglian herring before being requisitioned by the Admiralty on the outbreak of war in 1939. She became His Majesty's Boom Defence Vessel *Dundarg* and was stationed at Aultbea over on the west coast. Not having a boat to fish with, the Duthie family offered their services and were enlisted to crew the *Dundarg*. Her present owner has been reliably informed that something happened that led to her sustaining extensive damage to her keel upon rocks while back on the east coast. It was so severe, in fact, that apparently had it not been for the persistence of

Dundarg at Arbroath, 2020. (Simon Sawers)

the crew she would have been abandoned. *Dundarg* limped back to Fraserburgh and repairs were undertaken by Wilson Noble.

After the war, she returned to fishing and had a very prosperous career. She changed owners over the years, her name remaining although she was re-registered from FR1212 to PD97. (Both of these numbers can still be seen carved into her deck beams in the saloon.) She was re-engined with a Gardner 8L3 in the 1950s and relocated to Hartlepool. During the summer months, she would trawl for prawns off Torness in the Forth and would land into Eyemouth. Her licence was sold around 1983 and she was sold soon after.

But this wasn't the end for the 44-year-old boat. She was bought by a carpenter, who wanted to start a charter diving business. Over a couple of years, she was converted to accommodate twelve passengers and four crew. The Gardner was removed as the engine was pretty worn and the gearbox had lost its will to function. A new deckhouse was added, her bulwarks were replaced and masts and sails fitted. From 1985 to 2008 *Dundarg* took out countless divers, canoeists, sightseers, movie stars and anglers all over the west coast of Scotland, St Kilda, Isle of Man, Orkney and Shetland, and Norway.

There was one story I heard about her in the 1990s when in Oban. When working the west coast as a dive boat, she was skippered by a character called 'Cubby' (no further details). The boat was owned by a woman with an aristocratic-sounding name, although my source couldn't remember it. Nevertheless, he did mention that she had to skipper the boat when Cubby, as happened sometimes, went missing among the Oban hostelries!

In 1999 *Dundarg* was chartered to take part in a film celebrating the escapades of a Whitby man named Jack Lammiman, who defied the authorities and took his converted fishing boat to Jan Mayen Island in the Arctic Circle in order to place a commemorative plaque to his hero, Captain Scoresby. The movie was filmed between Whitby and Skye and starred several well-known British actors: Bob Hoskins, Sadie Frost and Maureen Lipman.

However, by 2008, *Dundarg* was tired, and in need of re-nailing and re-caulking. Her fit-out was dated and some of her machinery needed upgrading. Added to this, she had some damage internally from a fire caused by some defective electrics. She was advertised for sale and relocated to Wales, then to Northern Ireland and eventually back to Scotland.

Her present owner purchased her in about 2016 and has spent many hours, and pounds for that matter, restoring her, including taking her out of the water at Arbroath in July 2019, where much work was done to her hull. She remains an ongoing restoration.

WILSON NOBLE: *SOVEREIGN*, LH171

Sovereign was launched back in 1936 for Thomas Hall of Newhaven, although within three years she was requisitioned by the War Department for service between 1939 and 1945. After the war she was bought by Thomas Dawson and based in Seahouses under the registration BK29. Her original Kelvin J4 44hp engine was replaced with a Gardner 6LW in about 1955.

Over the next few years she changed hands and registrations (LH368, HL165), until she was bought by David W. Alexander and Edward Wood of Whitburn in 1969. The boat was based in North Shields and the two families worked her for some forty years, even after old Mr Alexander died at the helm. By 2009 she was in poor condition and nail rot almost saw her sink when a plank sprung at sea.

At 43ft in length, she was deemed perfect for working the ring-net as the deck allowed space for six to work, as did the accommodation. She would also work drift nets and seine nets at creel fishing, all at different times. The wheelhouse is the original size, even if has been rebuilt. In 1936 such a small wheelhouse was deemed big enough for the helmsman and the controls, especially as the men had previously helmed in the open.

Sovereign.

She was bought by her present owners, the Northumbrian Fishing Heritage Trust, and later restored by South Shields boatbuilder Fred Crowell. Today *Sovereign* remains almost true to when she was launched and is regarded as being the longest in-service fishing boat in the British fleet because, when she was de-registered in 2009, she had served for seventy-two years. She is based at St Peter's Marina, Newcastle, and is on the National Historic Ships Register.

WILSON NOBLE: HARVEST REAPER, FR235

Now lying ashore looking very sad at Burghead is the 46ft fifie-type fishing boat *Harvest Reaper*, FR235, built in 1931. She was powered by a 66hp Kelvin Ricardo diesel. She fished from Fraserburgh using small-line, great-line, herring drift net and seine net. Her skipper and owner was John Downie May until 1965, when his son Jimmy May took the helm.

During the war the vessel was involved in an incident at 11.20 a.m. on 29 April 1946, when she was 6 miles north-north-east off Fraserburgh. A Royal Navy Air Arm Firefly aircraft (MB734) used for training suffered a loss

Harvest Reaper at Burghead, 2021.

of power and ditched near the *Harvest Reaper*, breaking off the fishing boat's aft mast with its wing, before hitting the sea. Despite several attempts by the fishing boat crew to rescue the pilot, they were unable to save him. The aircraft was being flown from Naval Air Station Rattray by Sub-Lieutenant Kenneth David Williams, aged 20 from Liverpool.

Harvest Reaper was sold in 1974 to Stanley Lyon of Macduff and he re-registered her as BF214 and mainly worked the seine net with her. Ten years later she was registered WK43 and moved to Wick, where she also worked creels under the ownership of Alexander Gunn, Inverness. She was decommissioned in 1986 and was subsequently in private hands at Wick and later Burghead.

Harvest Reaper has, since 2015, stood ashore on the north side of Burghead, with only her hull remaining and her full-length almost vertical rudder and chain steering, her masts and wheelhouse having disappeared over time. I read recently of her being described as 'a miserable, rotting hulk … so-called heritage'. Having a look myself in the summer of 2021 during some research for this book, I can only concur with this description. As both Jimmy and John May told me, they'd have been better burning the vessel rather than leaving her to the elements.

James Noble: Harvest Reaper, FR177

Jimmy May decided that he had the need for a larger, more powerful, vessel. Replacing the old *Harvest Reaper* in 1974, he commissioned Jimmy Noble and later launched the transom-sterned *Harvest Reaper*, FR177, down the ways. John May, Jimmy's son, told me:

> She was a great boat, well-built and a good sea boat. My dad was skipper and my uncle was driver as he was a time-served engineer, so she was well looked after. We went to Jimmy Noble as we thought they built the best boat, and Jimmy's wife was my dad's cousin. She was fully shelter-decked in 1983 at Macduff.

She was sold to Tarbert in about 1997 to Gary, who had previously owned another J. Noble boat, *Duthies*, FR132, built the year before *Harvest Reaper*. She became TT177 before being sold to James Chown of Padstow and then becoming PW177. In December 2020 she was sold to Ireland.

John skippered the family boat until she was sold, although there are those who recall the heyday of the fishing. Albert Booth told me: 'That was a nice sea boat. I used to go out in it when I was a wee boy in the school holidays.

Jim May and his crew were very nice guys. My first pay packet was £50 in 1979. Times were good fun!'

Harvest Reaper, FR177. (Peter Drummond)

JAMES NOBLE: OCEAN PEARL, FR378

Ocean Pearl, FR378, is, at present, the oldest known survivor of the James Noble yard. Launched in 1933, she was of the small motorised fifie type, bauldie, half-Zulu or yawl, whatever takes your fancy name-wise! It's a difficult one and many of these smaller vessels were built on the Scottish east coast. They serve as a hybrid between the Zulu with its heavily raked sternpost and the upright fifie. The Zulu stern was found unsuitable for cutting out the propeller aperture post-motorisation, but to keep the keel short (harbour dues were paid on keel length), a smaller amount of rake was incorporated into the design. This became almost a template for small motorised vessels to work lines and the seine net in the 1920s and *Ocean Pearl* is an excellent example. Good sea boats they were, too.

    Ocean Pearl is under 40ft, which allowed her to fish within the 3-mile limit with nets and lines out of Peterhead. She was requisitioned in 1939 by the Admiralty and used as a naval supply vessel around Scapa Flow. After the war she went back into fishing for several years and in 1948 she was sold to J. William Tait, who worked her until 1967. He then sold her to Joseph Anthony Moore Phillips, father of Captain Mark Phillips, ex-husband to Princess Anne, who kept her based in Whitby. In 1981, three owners later, she arrived in Staines for restoration. Apart from some work replacing the stern apron, some lodging knees, some deck beams and most of the stanchions, work never progressed further after complaints from the owner's wife and mutterings of 'boat widow'! Thus she lay in a disused tarmac works next to the Penton Hook Marina boatyard, which they used as a 'resting place'.

TV producer Michael Custance spotted her there lying over on her side in 1996 and eventually bought her, thinking her worthy of saving. He transported her by road – after four police escorts because she exceeded the 3.5m width limit – to the Combes boatyard in Bosham, West Sussex, for restoration. But, due to pressure from a new business and ownership of the 40ft oyster boat *Four Rivers*, he was never to see the restoration. When Combes yard closed in 1999, *Ocean Pearl* was the only vessel left. Nick Gates, by then ex-slipway manager and soon-to-be-self-employed boatbuilder, was living in the yard at the time and he recalls how he would survey the boat over his bowl of Alpen each morning. In time he bought her for £500 and began a restoration of many years.

However, from the outset, he found a hull that he described as being pretty fair. Only where she'd been sitting on her side did

Stern view of *Ocean Pearl*, 2007.

rainwater cause significant damage to frames and larch planking. He removed the 3 tons of concrete ballast, exposing more rotten frames, and eventually replaced about half the framing. When she was then immersed in seawater, she was left to swell and more work resulted in planking being replaced, as well as the deck and deck beams, coach roof and internals. At the same time, he rigged her with two lugsails, taking a pattern from the Manx nobby *Gladys*, PL61, which he deemed capable of being sailed by two people. By 2005 he and his partner Ness were off to sail to the Isle of Wight. Today, although he's improved and lengthened the rig since I saw her in Looe in June 2007, they sail her widely. Pretty good after eighty-eight years and as much a testament to her original builders as it is to Nick Gates in his long-standing endeavours at her full restoration.

James Noble: Maureen, WK270

The 1963-built 55ft *Maureen* was commissioned by Thurso owner William Simpson and was considered to be a new style of seiner with increased power and fuller in shape to counteract this. She was named after the 12-year-old daughter of William, who was given a gold watch by James McDonald. According to the *Aberdeen Press and Journal* of 5 September 1963, McDonald had told the reporter that the prospects of new orders for the yard were remote at the time, although they had a few repair jobs that wouldn't keep the workforce going for long. The yard was employing twenty-five men. Nevertheless, it did launch three boats the following year, so things must have improved, perhaps given the success of the vessel.

For, soon after launch, she was noted as landing a good catch of 270 boxes of cod, which was deemed the best for over a year, realising over £80 for each share fisherman and £300 for the owner/skipper.

By 1979 she'd been bought by James MacDonald of Campbeltown and renamed *Crimson Arrow 4*, being registered CN155. A decade or so later she'd moved to Northern Ireland, owned by Albert Thomas Graham, retaining the same registry until the early 1990s, when she became N128.

By 2007 she was owned by Scott McDowall and based in Girvan as a trawler/scalloper, later being re-registered OB128. Malc Hutchison owned her for some time, having bought her in Mallaig. On 11 January 2015 she broke free from her mooring on Kerrera Island, off Oban, and drifted around the point, and onto the beach just under Dunollie Castle on the north side of Oban Bay. It was said that if she'd hit 50 yards either side of where she did, she'd have been a total loss. She wasn't, though, and was got off without too much damage.

By April 2018, tired and worn out, she was bought by John Wood who, along with his brother Billy, gave the boat a badly needed restoration lasting just over a year, so that by July 2019 she was back at sea. She's currently working as a twin-rig trawler, skippered by Bob Dunsire. Between the two brothers, they have a Facebook page dedicated to the vast amount of work they undertook on the vessel.

In Billy's words, she was:

special because we brought her back from the brink of going under the chainsaw after spending a large chunk of her career at the clams; she was just done. It was definitely a case of heart over head financially! The list of jobs is too long but she's been made seaworthy, no mean feat! Converted to twin rig. New hydraulic system. New engine and gearbox. Whaleback and shelter and hopper. Cabin galley and wheelhouse stripped out and renewed. Completely re-wired. As it is she must be one of the oldest Noble's boats still actively fishing and with the work done to her there's no reason we can't get another 20yrs out of her. I honestly believe boats have souls and stories to tell. In a throw away culture it's often easy to do what's easy and not what's right.

One response on the Facebook page was from Maureen Sinclair, the original 'Maureen':

Thanks for letting me join your group, very interested to see what you have done to this 57-year-old girl. My Dad William Simpson had the *Maureen* built by Noble in Fraserburgh in 1963. After he died in 1969 it was skippered by a few different people, then it was used for sea angling.

Today she's just *Crimson Arrow*, the '4' having been dropped, with the registration KY142. John has now bought the *Prevail*, SY121, a vessel built by Gerrards of Arbroath in 1990 as *Headway IV*, PD229. She became *Rebecca*, WY477, in 1995, then FR103 before going back to her original name and number, until she moved again back to England as *Katie Louise*, WY794, then *Kristanjo*, WY794, in 2002, then *Temeraire*, N850, in Kilkeel before becoming *Prevail*. She sank in Stornoway harbour and was another destined for the chainsaw until John got hold of her. Work progresses with a new name: *Crimson Sea*.

Crimson Arrow, N128, off Peel. (Darren Purves)

Goldseeker at Ullapool, 2021.

JAMES NOBLE: *GOLDSEEKER*

When the Department of Agriculture and Fisheries for Scotland wanted a new fishery research vessel in 1966, they turned to Jimmy Noble. However, if you look through the records of Marine Scotland, you see a pattern of using the coastal boatyards for the commissioning of new small vessels. The first fishery research/protection vessels were steam vessels, with the first *Goldseeker* being a 1900-built steam trawler. In 1924 they ordered the first new smaller vessel *Vaila* from Hugh MacLean of Govan, followed by one from J. N. Miller & Sons of St Monans in 1936. The same year saw another from Herd & Mackenzie and in 1947 they acquired the 1945-built MFV1195, which was renamed *Clupea*, the name giving away her task of overseeing the herring fishery! Then came another from Miller's in 1958, with the second *Goldseeker*, at 50ft, being the smallest to date and, in actuality, the last small wooden vessel in the Scottish fishery protection fleet.

In 1993 she was sold into private hands and it is believed that this was to a company called Ocean Seafare Ltd, which undertook survey and mooring work with her.

In about the mid-1990s another company bought the boat to service the Klondyke fleet in Shetland. *Goldseeker* went to Ullapool for some work, the low-pressure winch and gantry being taken off her and a Hiab crane fitted to her. After the demise of the Shetland Klondyke industry the boat went back to Ullapool.

The current owners acquired *Goldseeker* in 1999 and, at first, they did a few runs out for the Klondykers at Ullapool, as well as using the boat to do diving charters and to lay local moorings. In time, that was given up and the boat simply became a so-called pleasure vessel in which the owners were able to cruise the west coast and further afield. However, today she still has a feel of authenticity. Although she's not a working vessel any longer, on deck she retains complete originality from her klondyking days, while the accommodation has been modified to suit a cruising mode such as deckhouse with galley and seating, and a double bed in the forward part. The engine room, with the Gardner 6LX ticking away, is little changed except for some updating with pumps and generators. All in all, she is a reminder of how adaptable Jimmy Noble was, and, as a vintage vessel, given that the current owners keep on top of her upkeep, one that has many more years' life left in her.

5

Yard Lists
for Fishing Vessels by
Wilson Noble & Co.

1 *GOWAN*, FR232

Year Launched:	1907	First Owner:	A. Noble, R. Noble, A. McDonald & J. McDonald

Principal Dimensions:	
Length (ft)	90
Beam (ft)	19.5
Depth (ft)	8.9
GRT	97
Engine	J.S.Vaux (steam)
HP	31

History and Status:
1915: chartered to Irish Government & re-registered as LY49
1925: returned to owners & re-registered FR99
1929: renamed *Ident* & re-registered as PD47
1937: scrapped

2 *KINNAIRD*, FR205

Year Launched:	1907	First Owner:	Jas R. Gordon, Fraserburgh

Principal Dimensions:	
Length (ft)	85.5
Beam (ft)	19.4
Depth (ft)	9.5
GRT	94
Engine	Clyne & Mitchell (steam)
HP	22

The launch of the *Kinnaird*.

History and Status:
1920: registration cancelled and used as cargo vessel
1927: renamed *My Seal* & re-registered as INS125
1930: ran aground and wrecked in Loch Eport, North Uist

3 *RELY*

Year Launched:	1911	First Owner:	Fraserburgh

Principal Dimensions:	
Length (ft)	39.2
Beam (ft)	12.1
Depth (ft)	5.9
GRT	12
Engine	Kelvin
HP	15

History and Status:
Built as a pilot vessel
1955: registered as a converted pilot vessel
1972: owned by Lt Cmdr C.R. O'Brien, Oxted, Surrey. Home port Heybridge Basin

4 *VIOLET*, FR451

Violet, FR451, with the Forbes-built *Venture*, FR350, on the Fraserburgh pontoon.

Year Launched:	1911	First Owner:	Alexander Grieve Stephen, Fraserburgh

Principal Dimensions:	
Length (ft)	45.4
Beam (ft)	13.2
Depth (ft)	6.2
GRT	18.72
	Rigged with two lugsails at launch
Engine	Kelvin
HP	15

History and Status:
1975: re-registered as C132. Ceased fishing soon after and sold for private use
Crossed the Atlantic
By 1986 bought by third American owner and restored
2013: sold again to Chicago and still sailing

5 *VESPER*, FR453

Vesper, FR453, with Sandy Stephen.

Year Launched:	1911	First Owner:	George Noble and John Buchan

Principal Dimensions:	
Length (ft)	45.4
Beam (ft)	13.2
Depth (ft)	6.2
GRT	18.72
	Rigged with two lugsails at launch
Engine	Kelvin (1914)
HP	15

History and Status:
1970: re-registered as KY36
1983: re-registered as A36
1988: ceased fishing and sold to Roman Catholic priest
1989: sold again and funds required for restoration unforthcoming. Scrapped at Buckie

6 *ST JOHN III*, LY909

Year Launched:	1912	First Owner:	Denis & John Gallagher, Downings, Ireland

Principal Dimensions:	
Length (ft)	54.5
Beam (ft)	
Depth (ft)	
GRT	
Engine	
HP	

History and Status:
Built on Zulu lines for west coast of Ireland, cost £166
1915: sold for £80 + £75.5 for gear

7 *WHITE OAK*, FR558

Year Launched:	1913	First Owner:	T. May, Inverallochy & G. Chalmers, Fraserburgh

Principal Dimensions:	
Length (ft)	84.5
Beam (ft)	18.3
Depth (ft)	8.7
GRT	75
Engine	Lewis of Torry (steam)
HP	22

History and Status:
1918: sold & re-registered as BF523
1934: sold for scrap and broken up in Orkney

8 *VIOLET FLOWER*, PD148

Year Launched:	1914	First Owner:	T. Strachan, R. Irvin & J. Williamson, Fraserburgh

Principal Dimensions:	
Length (ft)	
Beam (ft)	
Depth (ft)	
GRT	36.0
Engine	(steam)
HP	

History and Status:
1947: scrapped

9 *MACKEREL SKY*

Year Launched:	1919	First Owner:	Admiralty

Principal Dimensions:	
Length (ft)	87.6
Beam (ft)	19.7
Depth (ft)	9.7
GRT	92
Engine	Beardmore (steam)
HP	43

The Admiralty steam drifter *Mackerel Sky* as *Headway*, FR37.

History and Status:
1921: renamed *Drainie* & registered as INS365
1945: renamed *Headway* & re-registered as FR37
1951: scrapped

10 *MILKY WAY*, BF334

Steam drifter
Milky Way,
BF334.

Year Launched:	1919	First Owner:	Admiralty

Principal Dimensions:	
Length (ft)	86.8
Beam (ft)	19.9
Depth (ft)	9.8
GRT	92.0
Engine	Beardmore (steam)
HP	42

History and Status:
1920: re-registered as BF336
1937: renamed *Boyds* & re-registered as FR294
1951: scrapped at Fraserburgh

11 *EVANGELINE*, FR729

Evangeline, FR163, after her stern had been chopped off to shorten the vessel.

Year Launched:	1920	First Owner:	L. Buchan, Fraserburgh

Principal Dimensions:	
Length (ft)	46.5
Beam (ft)	14.0
Depth (ft)	6.9
GRT	20.0
Engine	Kelvin
HP	15

History and Status:
1926: re-registered as TT26, based in Carradale (February)
1926: re-registered as CN172 (December)
1947: re-registered as FR163
1967: re-registered as LK622
1975: re-registered as LK182, later DE26
c. 1995: ceased fishing and sold into private ownership
1986: ceased fishing
1998: caught fire and later scrapped on Anstruther's pier

12 *VILLAGE MAID*, FR142

Village Maid, FR142, as LK3 alongside *Baltasound Pier*. (Willie Mouat)

Year Launched:	1920	First Owner:	W. Noble, Fraserburgh

Principal Dimensions:	
Length (ft)	46.0
Beam (ft)	14.0
Depth (ft)	6.5
GRT	18.84
Engine	Kelvin
HP	44

History and Status:
1925: re-registered as TT21
1944: re-registered as CN35
1947: re-registered as INS46
1949: re-registered as LK3
1957: sold for £600
1963: re-registered as K850,
1963: sank off White Head, Loch Eriboll, Sutherland. Crew rescued by Aberdeen trawler *Mount Everest*

13 *CORBIEHILL*

Year Launched:	1922	First Owner:	Consortium of FR businessmen as Fraserburgh Shipping Co.

Principal Dimensions:	
Length (ft)	99.2
Beam (ft)	22.9
Depth (ft)	10.9
GRT	167.0
Engine	2 × Gardner
HP	2 × 90

History and Status:
Built to transport empty herring barrels
1924: sold to Wick & renamed *Millrock*
1931: sold to Norway
1958: renamed *Andvag*

14 *BRITANNIA*, LK140

Year Launched:	1922	First Owner:	A. Fullerton, Lerwick

Principal Dimensions:	
Length (ft)	37.4
Beam (ft)	12.9
Depth (ft)	5.7
GRT	12.83
Engine	Atlantic
HP	40

History and Status:
1959: scrapped

15 *ELSIE WOOD*, LK303

Year Launched:	1923	First Owner:	Lerwick

Principal Dimensions:	
Length (ft)	39.0
Beam (ft)	13.6
Depth (ft)	7.0
GRT	16.71
Engine	Gardner
HP	25

Budding Rose, LK303, at Scalloway, 1932.

History and Status:
1930: renamed *Budding Rose*, LK303 at Burra
1947: owned by Lowestoft Herring Drifters Ltd & others
1955: ceased fishing

16 *ECLIPSE*, LK287

Year Launched:	1923	First Owner:	W. Watt, Lerwick

Principal Dimensions:	
Length (ft)	38.0
Beam (ft)	9.0
Depth (ft)	5.2
GRT	8.0
Engine	Kelvin
HP	30

History and Status:
1979: ceased fishing

17 *UTILITY*, A950

Year Launched:	1923	First Owner:	A. Leiper, Aberdeen

Principal Dimensions:	
Length (ft)	39.8
Beam (ft)	13.9
Depth (ft)	7.5
GRT	18.67
Engine	Kelvin
HP	60

History and Status:
1937: re-registered as WK276
1941: re-registered as A187
1953: re-registered as FR362
1965: wrecked

18 *GOLDEN RAY*, BF44

Year Launched:	1924	First Owner:	F. Watt, Gardenstown

Principal Dimensions:	
Length (ft)	45.0
Beam (ft)	14.8
Depth (ft)	5.5
GRT	18.48
Engine	Kelvin
HP	60

Golden Ray, BF44, as *Freedom*, LK461.

History and Status:
Re-registered as OB93
Renamed *Freedom*, LK461
Renamed *Fair Dawn*
1974: wrecked

19 *MARY MANSON*, OB9

Year Launched:	1924	First Owner:	J. Manson, Mallaig

Principal Dimensions:	
Length (ft)	41.3
Beam (ft)	14.0
Depth (ft)	4.3
GRT	11.19
Engine	Kelvin
HP	30

Deck view of *Mary Manson* alongside *Margaret Ann*, OB78.

History and Status:
1948: renamed *Jessie Alice*
1950s: renamed *Winner*
1966: wrecked

20 *GLEANER*, BF88

Year Launched:	1925	First Owner:	J.R. Lovie, Whitehills

Principal Dimensions:	
Length (ft)	35.0
Beam (ft)	11.5
Depth (ft)	5.0
GRT	9.05
Engine	Kelvin
HP	30

History and Status:
1935: re-registered as WK63
1954: re-registered as INS208
1961: ceased fishing

21 *THALASSA*, CN112

Year Launched:	1926	First Owner:	D. McIntosh, Carradale

Principal Dimensions:	
Length (ft)	43.0
Beam (ft)	14.3
Depth (ft)	6.9
GRT	14.64
Engine	Kelvin
HP	30

History and Status:
Re-registered as ME124
Renamed *Sisters*, BRD410

22 *PARAGON*, CN117

Year Launched:	1926	First Owner:	D. McIntosh, Carradale

Principal Dimensions:	
Length (ft)	43.0
Beam (ft)	13.0
Depth (ft)	5.8
GRT	14.66
Engine	Gleniffer
HP	32

Paragon, CN117, alongside at *Tarbert* (nearest to quay), with other shark catchers including *Perseverance*, CN152, which belonged to the author in 1990–95.

History and Status:
1946: bought by Anthony Watkins as part of his basking shark catching vessel fleet
1950: sold

23 *MAID OF HONOUR*, CN120

Year Launched:	1926	First Owner:	D. Campbell, Carradale

Principal Dimensions:	
Length (ft)	43.2
Beam (ft)	13.0
Depth (ft)	5.8
GRT	14.66
Engine	Gleniffer
HP	32

History and Status:
1946: re-registered as WK106
1949: re-registered as LK81
1955: burnt

24 *FAIRY QUEEN*, CN128

Year Launched:	1926	First Owner:	J. Robertson, Campbeltown

Principal Dimensions:	
Length (ft)	43.0
Beam (ft)	130
Depth (ft)	5.8
GRT	14.99
Engine	Kelvin
HP	30

Fairy Queen, CN128, registered as K823, in the Vat of Kirbister, Stronsay.

History and Status:
1947: re-registered as WK204
1961: re-registered as INS127, K823, BRD6
2009: reported still afloat at Galway

25 *HAPPY DAYS*

Year Launched:	1926	First Owner:	Unknown

Principal Dimensions:	
Length (ft)	38.0
Beam (ft)	8.0
Depth (ft)	4.0
GRT	8.0
Engine	2 × Perkins
HP	

History and Status:
Built as a yacht first registered in Whitby
1930: owned by Laurence Smales, Sleights, Yorks
1972: owned by Argyll Arms Hotel, Campbeltown, Argyll

26 *SWIFTWING 2*, BCK82

Year Launched:	1926	First Owner:	A. Mair, Buckie

Principal Dimensions:	
Length (ft)	52.2
Beam (ft)	16.3
Depth (ft)	7.0
GRT	26.8
Engine	Kelvin
HP	60

Swiftwing 2, BCK82, in Shetland as LK192.

History and Status:
1947: was in Lerwick, registered as LK192
1970: was in Out Skerries, Shetland, then Walls
1979: ceased fishing and used as flit boat for the Whalsay Fish Factory
Perhaps back to Walls then eventually broke loose from mooring and ran ashore at Burwick, north of Scalloway

27 *BREADWINNER*, AH20

Year Launched:	1927	First Owner:	T. Beattie, Arbroath

Principal Dimensions:	
Length (ft)	43.5
Beam (ft)	14.1
Depth (ft)	7.3
GRT	16.85
Engine	
HP	

History and Status:
Renamed *Emulate*, LH24
1951: sold to England

28 *LILY*, ME22

Year Launched:	1927	First Owner:	J. Christie, Gourdon

Principal Dimensions:	
Length (ft)	37.5
Beam (ft)	12.2
Depth (ft)	5.8
GRT	11.95
Engine	
HP	

History and Status:
Renamed *Rimic*, BU35

29 *STELLA MARIS*, CN198

Year Launched:	1927	First Owner:	J. McIntosh, Carradale

Principal Dimensions:	
Length (ft)	43.0
Beam (ft)	13.0
Depth (ft)	5.8
GRT	14.95
Engine	Kelvin
HP	30

History and Status:
Re-registered as KY116
1947: re-registered as WK299
1950: renamed *St. Rognvald* & re-registered as LH50

30 *PILOT ME*, BF392

Year Launched:	1928	First Owner:	A. Paterson, Macduff

Principal Dimensions:	
Length (ft)	38.6
Beam (ft)	13.5
Depth (ft)	6.5
GRT	15.24
Engine	Kelvin
HP	44

Pilot Me, BF392.

History and Status:
1947: sold to Whitehills
1974: sold to Sittingbourne, Kent
1979: sold to Twickenham and converted for pleasure

31 *LINDFAR*, BK234

Year Launched:	1928	First Owner:	John M. Scott, Kew & John M. Holmes, Berwick

Principal Dimensions:	
Length (ft)	56.7
Beam (ft)	18.6
Depth (ft)	7.15
GRT	39.7
Engine	
HP	15

Lindfar, BK234, as *Rival 2*, WK123, about 1959.

History and Status:
1935: renamed *Prospecto* & re-registered as BK201
1948: renamed *Rival* & re-registered as WK123
2008: reported to be in Essex

32 *WINNER*, BF391

Year Launched:	1928	First Owner:	A. Gardiner, Cullen

Principal Dimensions:	
Length (ft)	38.6
Beam (ft)	13.5
Depth (ft)	6.5
GRT	15.24
Engine	Kelvin
HP	30

Winner, BF391

History and Status:
1954: renamed *Aultmore* & re-registered as A189
1962: renamed *Uberous* & re-registered as PD68
1984: ceased fishing

33 *MARY DUNCAN*, OB6

Year Launched:	1929	First Owner:	G. Duncan, Mallaig

Principal Dimensions:	
Length (ft)	51.4
Beam (ft)	15.4
Depth (ft)	7.1
GRT	25.29
Engine	
HP	

History and Status:
Renamed *Bonnie Ann*, N189
1947: re-registered as B252
1972: sunk off Kirkcudbrightshire coast. Crew rescued by helicopter

34 *IRMA*, CN45

Year Launched:	1929	First Owner:	J. Campbell, Carradale

Principal Dimensions:	
Length (ft)	45.8
Beam (ft)	14.3
Depth (ft)	6.3
GRT	18.57
Engine	Kelvin
HP	30

History and Status:
1960: sold and converted to pleasure

35 *BETTY*, INS48

Year Launched:	1929	First Owner:	W. McLennan, Avoch

Principal Dimensions:	
Length (ft)	42.0
Beam (ft)	14.0
Depth (ft)	6.0
GRT	15.88
Engine	Kelvin
HP	30

History and Status:
1967: renamed *Crest* & re-registered as BRD124
1991: ceased fishing

36 *GUIDING STAR*, LK43

Year Launched:	1929	First Owner:	A. Watt, Lerwick

Principal Dimensions:	
Length (ft)	33.0
Beam (ft)	11.4
Depth (ft)	4.0
GRT	6.53
Engine	Kelvin
HP	30

History and Status:
Re-registered as K843, BRD11, A315

37 *FLORA MACDONALD*, BRD33

Year Launched:	1929	First Owner:	R. McInnes, Portree

Principal Dimensions:	
Length (ft)	41.0
Beam (ft)	13.0
Depth (ft)	6.6
GRT	16.1
Engine	Kelvin
HP	30

History and Status:
1961: sank

38 *HARVESTER*, WK31

Year Launched:	1929	First Owner:	A. Cowie, Helmsdale

Principal Dimensions:	
Length (ft)	43.8
Beam (ft)	14.0
Depth (ft)	6.6
GRT	18.21
Engine	Gardner
HP	48

Time for a lick of paint for *Harvester*, WK31.

History and Status:
1967: re-registered as SA6

39 *GLEANER*, FR33

Year Launched:	1929	First Owner:	G. Duthie, Fraserburgh

Principal Dimensions:	
Length (ft)	45.4
Beam (ft)	14.3
Depth (ft)	6.7
GRT	19.57
Engine	Gardner
HP	36

History and Status:
1947: re-registered as INS66
1951: renamed *Kilda* & re-registered as SY346
1968: re-registered as BRD171
1973: sank

40 *VALHALLA*, OB51

Year Launched:	1930	First Owner:	A. Duncan, Mallaig

Principal Dimensions:	
Length (ft)	51.0
Beam (ft)	15.0
Depth (ft)	4.8
GRT	17.77
Engine	Kelvin
HP	60

History and Status:
1943: sold to Ministry of War Transport

41 *BOUNTEOUS SEA*, FR77

Year Launched:	1930	First Owner:	A. Third, Fraserburgh

Principal Dimensions:	
Length (ft)	69.6
Beam (ft)	20.0
Depth (ft)	7.3
GRT	30.03
Engine	Bolinder
HP	90

History and Status:
1956: re-registered as PD170

42 *NEWHAVEN*, LH54

Year Launched:	1930	First Owner:	T. Carnie, Newhaven

Principal Dimensions:	
Length (ft)	36.5
Beam (ft)	13.2
Depth (ft)	6.4
GRT	13.88
Engine	
HP	

History and Status:
Renamed *Adoration*, BA130
1973: sold and converted for pleasure

43 *PAL O'MINE*, FR158

Year Launched:	1930	First Owner:	W. Noble, Fraserburgh

Principal Dimensions:	
Length (ft)	33.7
Beam (ft)	11.7
Depth (ft)	5.7
GRT	10.11
Engine	Kelvin
HP	30

History and Status:
1965: sold to England & re-registered F40

44 *MIZPAH 3*, INS118

Year Launched:	1930	First Owner:	G. Jack, Avoch

Principal Dimensions:	
Length (ft)	43.6
Beam (ft)	14.9
Depth (ft)	6.6
GRT	20.46
Engine	
HP	

History and Status:
1946: re-registered as PD241
1947: re-registered as KY199
1954: renamed *Oor Lass* & re-registered as A36
1958: renamed *Our Lass* & re-registered as WK104
1958: caught fire and deliberately grounded at the Old Haven, Clyth. Crew could not extinguish fire and abandoned vessel

45 *HARVEST REAPER*, FR235

Year Launched:	1931	First Owner:	J.D. May

Principal Dimensions:	
Length (ft)	45.5
Beam (ft)	15.0
Depth (ft)	6.5
GRT	19.96
Engine	Kelvin
HP	30

Harvest Reaper.

History and Status:
1976: re-registered as BF214
1985: re-registered as WK43
1986: decommissioned
2018: put ashore at Burghead

46 *SNOWDROP*, LK242

Year Launched:	1931	First Owner:	J. Watt, Lerwick

Principal Dimensions:	
Length (ft)	45.5
Beam (ft)	14.5
Depth (ft)	7.5
GRT	22.27
Engine	
HP	

Snowdrop, LK242, alongside the quay at Stromness.

History and Status:
1990: registration cancelled

47 *STAR OF BETHLEHEM*, ME145

Year Launched:	1931	First Owner:	A. Stewart, Gourdon

Principal Dimensions:	
Length (ft)	34.7
Beam (ft)	11.7
Depth (ft)	5.6
GRT	10.0
Engine	Kelvin
HP	30

History and Status:
Re-registered as A96, ME10
Renamed Ebenezer, AH52
Renamed *Star of Bethlehem 2*, OB359
Renamed *Galatea*, CY60
Renamed *Skua*, SY216
Renamed *Venture*

48 *SILVER GREY*, CN235

Year Launched:	1932	First Owner:	A.D. Monair, Campbeltown

Principal Dimensions:	
Length (ft)	48.2
Beam (ft)	14.5
Depth (ft)	6.2
GRT	19.5
Engine	Gleniffer
HP	80

History and Status:
1942: renamed *Plough 2* & re-registered as KY190
1947: renamed *Silver Lassie* & re-registered as SH74
1951: renamed *Frank Albert* & re-registered as GY196
1953: renamed *Falcon II* & re-registered as SH153
1953: re-registered as WY94

49 *NOBLES*, CN236

Year Launched:	1932	First Owner:	J. Daniels, Campbeltown

Principal Dimensions:	
Length (ft)	48.2
Beam (ft)	14.5
Depth (ft)	6.2
GRT	19.5
Engine	
HP	

History and Status:
1960: registry cancelled

50 *JESSIE*, INS228

Jessie, INS228, steaming into Lossiemouth.

Year Launched:	1932	First Owner:	D. Jack, Avo

Principal Dimensions:	
Length (ft)	46.3
Beam (ft)	14.7
Depth (ft)	6.8
GRT	20.83
Engine	Kelvin
HP	66

History and Status:
1936: re-registered as TT94
1950: renamed *Guiding Star* & re-registered as RO47, CN96
1989: re-registered as WO149
1996: ceased fishing

51 *GOOD HOPE*, PD213

Year Launched:	1932	First Owner:	J. Duthie, Peterhead

Principal Dimensions:	
Length (ft)	48.0
Beam (ft)	16.5
Depth (ft)	6.5
GRT	26.45
Engine	Kelvin
HP	66

History and Status:
1935: re-registered as KY165
1947: renamed *Good Hope* & re-registered as BK87, AH87
1967: re-registered as KY365
1969: re-registered as AH18
1981: sank

52 *BARBARA*, INS571

Year Launched:	1933	First Owner:	G. Ralph, Nairn

Principal Dimensions:	
Length (ft)	45.5
Beam (ft)	
Depth (ft)	
GRT	18.6
Engine	
HP	

History and Status:
1937: sold to Dublin

53 *HAZAEL*, FR368

Year Launched:	1933	First Owner:	J. May, Fraserburgh

Principal Dimensions:	
Length (ft)	47.9
Beam (ft)	14.8
Depth (ft)	7.0
GRT	22.33
Engine	Kelvin
HP	66

History and Status:
1969: re-registered as LO2

54 *REUL NA MAIDNE*, CY349

Year Launched:	1933	First Owner:	J. McLeod, Isle of Barra

Principal Dimensions:	
Length (ft)	51.5
Beam (ft)	15.6
Depth (ft)	7.3
GRT	26.39
Engine	
HP	

History and Status:
1977: derelict

55 *BRIAR*, FR48

Year Launched:	1934	First Owner:	W.S. Buchan, Fraserburgh

Principal Dimensions:	
Length (ft)	55.6
Beam (ft)	17.5
Depth (ft)	6.4
GRT	24.95
Engine	Kelvin
HP	88

Briar, FR48.

History and Status:
1977: sold to Grimsby
Subsequently converted to yacht and sailed to Brisbane, Australia

56 *SOVEREIGN*, LH171

Year Launched:	1936	First Owner:	T. Hall, Newhaven

Principal Dimensions:	
Length (ft)	43.4
Beam (ft)	14.5
Depth (ft)	6.3
GRT	17.84
Engine	Kelvin
HP	44

Sovereign, LH171, as HL105.

History and Status:
1945: re-registered as BK29
1960: re-registered as LH368
1967: re-registered as HL165
2009: ceased fishing and rebuilt by owners. Boat on the National Historic Ships Register

57 *ENTERPRISE*, INS293

Year Launched:	1937	First Owner:	W. Duggie, Nairn

Principal Dimensions:	
Length (ft)	47.0
Beam (ft)	15.75
Depth (ft)	6.0
GRT	19.99
Engine	Kelvin
HP	44

History and Status:
1960: sold to Ireland

58 *BALMORAL*, INS314

Year Launched:	1937	First Owner:	D. Wallace, Nairn

Principal Dimensions:	
Length (ft)	58.0
Beam (ft)	17.0
Depth (ft)	7.1
GRT	27.57
Engine	Gardner
HP	102

History and Status:
1951: ran aground in thick fog near Strathy Point on the north coast of Sutherland. Crew were able to scramble ashore before she sank

59 *MAYFLOWER*, FR310

Year Launched:	1937	First Owner:	J. Runcie, Fraserburgh

Principal Dimensions:	
Length (ft)	69.25
Beam (ft)	18.75
Depth (ft)	9.16
GRT	53.52
Engine	53.52
HP	102

Mayflower, FR310, about to be launched from the yard. (Maureen Small)

History and Status:
1958: ran aground and wrecked on rocks at Cairnbulg. Crew rescued by Fraserburgh lifeboat and fishing boat *Gemini*

60 *MAY QUEEN*, LH196

Year Launched:	1937	First Owner:	A. Rutherford, Newhaven

Principal Dimensions:	
Length (ft)	45.7
Beam (ft)	15.4
Depth (ft)	6.5
GRT	20.59
Engine	Kelvin
HP	44

May Queen, LH196, at Dunbar. She was the only boat with electric start at the time.

History and Status:
Unknown

61 *COMFORT*, FR965

Year Launched:	1937	First Owner:	J. Noble, Fraserburgh

Principal Dimensions:	
Length (ft)	69.2
Beam (ft)	19.2
Depth (ft)	10.1
GRT	60.39
Engine	Kelvin
HP	132

History and Status:
1940: sunk in collision after being rammed in error by HMS *Lydd* off Dover, May 1940. Crew of six lost

62 *PERSEVERE*, LH204

Year Launched:	1937	First Owner:	William Liston & others, Newhaven

Principal Dimensions:	
Length (ft)	49.0
Beam (ft)	15.5
Depth (ft)	6.5
GRT	20.0
Engine	Kelvin
HP	66

History and Status:
Unknown

63 *PLOUGH*, BF82

Year Launched:	1938	First Owner:	W. Mair, Portsoy

Principal Dimensions:	
Length (ft)	30.7
Beam (ft)	10.7
Depth (ft)	4.5
GRT	6.65
Engine	Kelvin
HP	15

History and Status:
1952: re-registered as PD220
1963: re-registered as FR228, WK369, UL76

64 *PROMOTE 2*, FR420

Year Launched:	1938	First Owner:	A. Duthie, Fraserburgh

Principal Dimensions:	
Length (ft)	30.6
Beam (ft)	10.8
Depth (ft)	4.7
GRT	6.99
Engine	Kelvin
HP	22

History and Status:
1964: sold to Arbroath

65 *CHRISTMAS ROSE*, BF366

Year Launched:	1938	First Owner:	J. Napier, Whitehills

Principal Dimensions:	
Length (ft)	39.8
Beam (ft)	13.8
Depth (ft)	6.0
GRT	14.83
Engine	Kelvin
HP	66

Christmas Rose, BF366.

History and Status:
1975: ceased fishing

66 *HARMONY*, FR416

Year Launched:	1938	First Owner:	A. Noble, Fraserburgh

Principal Dimensions:	
Length (ft)	61.3
Beam (ft)	17.8
Depth (ft)	7.5
GRT	41.0
Engine	Gardner
HP	102

History and Status:
1962: sold to New Zealand

67 *BUDDING ROSE*, LK499

Year Launched:	1938	First Owner:	G. F. Smith, Whiteness

Principal Dimensions:	
Length (ft)	45.0
Beam (ft)	15.3
Depth (ft)	6.9
GRT	21.8
Engine	Kelvin
HP	66

History and Status:
1966: sold to Ireland & re-registered as D419

68 *BRIAR ROSE*, FR67

Year Launched:	1939	First Owner:	W. Buchan, Fraserburgh

Principal Dimensions:	
Length (ft)	60.8
Beam (ft)	18.7
Depth (ft)	8.75
GRT	49.32
Engine	Kelvin
HP	132

History and Status:
1971: re-registered as PL18
1978: broken up

69 *DUNDARG*, FR121

Year Launched:	1939	First Owner:	J. Duthie, Rosehearty

Principal Dimensions:	
Length (ft)	69.3
Beam (ft)	19.0
Depth (ft)	9.0
GRT	56.29
Engine	Kelvin
HP	132

Dundarg, FR121, at Great Yarmouth. Today she resides at Eyemouth.

History and Status:
1969: re-registered as PD97
1974: sold to England
1985: converted for holidays afloat
2008: sold to Wales, then Northern Ireland, then Scotland
2016: bought by present owner and undergoing restoration

70 *JEANNIE WEST*, FR146

Year Launched:	1939	First Owner:	J. Duthie, Fraserburgh

Principal Dimensions:	
Length (ft)	31.2
Beam (ft)	11.1
Depth (ft)	5.2
GRT	8.1
Engine	Kelvin
HP	22

Jeannie West, FR146.

History and Status:
1969: sold to the Isle of Man

71 *GIRL JEAN*, FR164

Girl Jean, FR164, as *Shepherd Boy*, FR428. She was ultimately dismantled in Anglesey.

Year Launched:	1939	First Owner:	W. Cardno, Fraserburgh

Principal Dimensions:	
Length (ft)	25.25
Beam (ft)	9.5
Depth (ft)	4.0
GRT	4.32
Engine	Kelvin
HP	15

History and Status:
1957: renamed *Shepherd Boy*, PD206, FR428
1974: sold to Wales
1990s: in Abersoch and sold to Anglesey
2000: dismantled

72 *GIRL DAISY*, PD

Girl Daisy as *Lorna Marie*, FD255.

(Note: It is possible that J. & G. Forbes built this vessel)

Year Launched:	1940	First Owner:	Bisset B. Coull, Peterhead

Principal Dimensions:	
Length (ft)	59.8
Beam (ft)	17.7
Depth (ft)	8.2
GRT	40.12
Engine	Gardner
HP	114

History and Status:
1948: re-registered as BF280
1951: re-registered as FR198
1953: renamed *Silver Gain* & re-registered as BF419
1956: re-registered as BK79
1973: renamed *Lorna Marie* & re-registered as FD255
1980s: de-registered

ADMIRALTY MOTOR MINESWEEPERS

A typical Admiralty Motor
Minesweeper as built by Wilson Noble
and many other UK yards.

The typical larger Admiralty Motor
Minesweeper of 140ft.

Principal Dimensions:	
Length (ft)	119.0
Beam (ft)	23.0
Depth (ft)	9.5
HP	500

Principal Dimensions:	
Length (ft)	139.8
Beam (ft)	26.0
Depth (ft)	9.5
HP	500

73	MMS10 (1939)
74	MMS11 (1940)
75	MMS18 (1940)
76	MMS34 (1940)
77	MMS35 (1940)
78	MMS56 (1941)
79	MMS57 (1941)
80	MMS133 (1941)
81	MMS134 (1941)
82	MMS188 (1942)
83	MMS189 (1942)
84	MMS215 (1942)
85	MMS219 (1942)
86	MMS277 (1943)
87	MMS301 (1943)
88	MMS306 (1943)
89	MMS307 (1943)

90	MMS1021 (1944)
91	MMS1048 (1944)
92	MMS1049 (1945)

ADMIRALTY MOTOR FISHING VESSELS

Boy James, PD410, built for the Admiralty in 1946.

Principal Dimensions:	
Length (ft)	75.5
Beam (ft)	19.8
Depth (ft)	5.5
Engine	Lister Blackstone
HP	160

93	MFV1017 (1944)	(sold to Hong Kong)
94	MFV1054 (1945)	(sold to Singapore)
95	MFV1127 (1945)	(sold to Hong Kong)
96	MFV1128 (1945)	(sold to Guernsey)
97	MFV1129 (1946)	(sold to Borneo)
98	MFV1130 (1946)	(sold to Singapore)
99	MFV1215 (1946)	(converted to pleasure: *Blue Lizard*)
100	MFV1216 (1946)	(renamed *Boy James* & registered as PD410, then *Excelsior*, FR249)
101	MFV1217 (1946)	(renamed *Mary Watt* & registered as LK367)
102	MFV1228 (1946)	(unknown)

MFVs variously sold after the war as in brackets above.

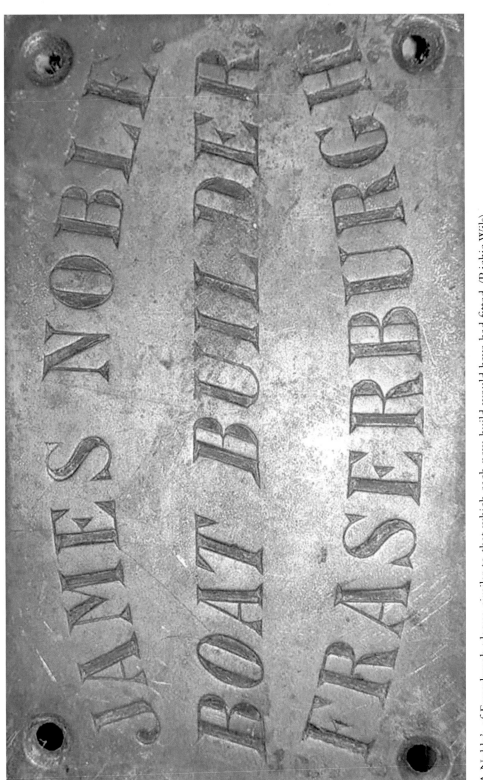

A Noble's of Fraserburgh plaque, similar to that which each new-build would have had fitted. (Richie Wils)

The small Zulu *Violet*, FR451, coming alongside the yawl *Fragrance*.

Pilot Me, BF392, launched in 1928.

Brighter Hope, FR371, at Voe, Shetland; said to be the first boat to fish Bergen banks at the seine net under her skipper/owner Sandy Watt.

Watchful, BF107, the last boat built by Wilson Noble in 1958.

Florentine, CN197, off Carradale in 1959, not long before she was sold and replaced by *Mallaig Mhor*, built by Noble's in 1947 and which was renamed *Florentine* and registered CN7. It was then fished successfully at the ring net throughout the 1960s to the mid-1970s by the three MacConnachie brothers, James, John, and Walter. (Lachie Paterson)

Ocean Pearl sailing at Looe in 2007. (Author)

Watercress in the burn at Waterfoot, Carradale. (Lachie Paterson)

Oak Lea, OB74, alongside *Supreme*, PD190, at Kyleakin with the ruins of Castle Moil behind.

Deck view of the
Carradale ringer
Queen of the Fleet,
CN269, with its lovely
varnished hull.

Primrose: Danny (back to camera), George (yellow oilskins) and Willie Skinner (skipper) in the
wheelhouse. (Iain Smith)

Saint Maughold alongside at Peel. (Mike Craine)

Maid of Erin at Port Askaig, Islay.

The coble *Angela May* at Filey.

Maureen, as *Crimson Arrow*, KY142, coming into Pittenweem, June 2021. (John Wood)

Heather Maid at the Ramsey shipyard slip prior to scrapping in 2020. (Archie Purves)

Faithful as *Golden Hope*, LH384, at Eyemouth. (Colin Watt)

Cynosure, A774.

Ocean Harvester off Peel. (Darren Purves)

New Dawn, PL1, coming into Peel. (Darren Purves)

Jann Denise, the last cruiser-sterned vessel built by Noble's. (Darren Purves)

Edelweiss and *Fruitful Harvest* alongside each other, being fitted out. (Ken and Duncan Cregeen)

Stern view of *Edelweiss*, 1972. The vessel suffered five broken frames on launch because the engine was mounted forward. Jimmy was heard to say he'd never launch like that again! (Ken and Duncan Cregeen)

Fruitful Harvest being fitted out in 1972. Note the two yawls against the quay. Noble's yard lies to the extreme right of the photo. (Ken and Duncan Cregeen)

The ferry *Lochaber* presumed to have been the ferry built for the Corran ferry crossing on Loch Linnhe. (Maureen and Bruce Herd)

Duthies as *Silver Fern*, MT99, out of the water in 2021. (John Andrea Mcavoy)

The launch of the *Harvest Reaper*, FR177, in 1974.

Golden Fleece being fitted out alongside the quay in 1975.

Devotion hitting the water.

Jasper 2, the last wooden new-build launched into Fraserburgh, just after her launch celebrations.

Jimmy Noble in about 1980.

103 *PALM TREE*, FR43

Year Launched:	1947	First Owner:	F. Stephen, Fraserburgh

Principal Dimensions:	
Length (ft)	58.0
Beam (ft)	17.3
Depth (ft)	7.6
GRT	34.73
Engine	Kelvin
HP	88

History and Status:
Became *Provider*
1963: sold to England

104 *WESTBURN*, FR170

Year Launched:	1947	First Owner:	G. West, Fraserburgh

Principal Dimensions:	
Length (ft)	70.0
Beam (ft)	19.4
Depth (ft)	6.8
GRT	38.05
Engine	Gardner
HP	114

Westburn, FR170, the second vessel built after the war ended, here as N171.

History and Status:
1968: re-registered as N171
1975: flooded and sank in Irish Sea off St Bee's Head

105 *GOLDEN HARVEST*, FR124

Year Launched:	1947	First Owner:	G. Summers, Fraserburgh

Principal Dimensions:	
Length (ft)	72.0
Beam (ft)	19.4
Depth (ft)	6.8
GRT	37.99
Engine	Gardner
HP	152

Golden Harvest, FR124, as PD263.

History and Status:
1953: re-registered as PD263
1972: sold to Northern Ireland

106 *TORFNESS*, INS164

Year Launched:	1947	First Owner:	D. Main, Burghead

Principal Dimensions:	
Length (ft)	67.0
Beam (ft)	19.3
Depth (ft)	8.6
GRT	45.71
Engine	Blackstone
HP	160

Stern view of *Torfness*. It is probable that she was scrapped at Dunmore East.

History and Status:
1987: sold to Ireland & re-registered as D378
2000: ceased fishing

107 *HAZAEL 3*, FR107

Year Launched:	1947	First Owner:	W. Reid, Fraserburgh

Principal Dimensions:	
Length (ft)	72.0
Beam (ft)	19.5
Depth (ft)	8.7
GRT	49.78
Engine	Gardner
HP	152

History and Status:
1968: sold to Ireland & re-registered as D482
1968: wrecked when ran aground near entrance to Waterford harbour

108 *META BRUCE*, BCK195

Year Launched:	1948	First Owner:	J. Bruce, Buckie

Principal Dimensions:	
Length (ft)	70.0
Beam (ft)	19.2
Depth (ft)	8.7
GRT	49.61
Engine	Blackstone
HP	160

Meta Bruce, BCK195, coming into Fraserburgh.

History and Status:
1963: sold to Ireland & re-registered as D195
2005: derelict at Clonderalaw Bay, near Knock, Co. Clare

109 *GOLDEN FEATHER*, FR225

Year Launched:	1948	First Owner:	J. Blackhall, Fraserburgh

Principal Dimensions:	
Length (ft)	71.0
Beam (ft)	19.5
Depth (ft)	8.8
GRT	49.42
Engine	Gardner
HP	152

Golden Feather, FR225.

History and Status:
1971: sold to Ireland & re-registered as W225
1999: ceased fishing & subsequently laid up for several years and eventually scuttled

110 *SILVER SPRAY*, FR226

Year Launched:	1948	First Owner:	A. Cardno, Cairnbulg

Principal Dimensions:	
Length (ft)	70.0
Beam (ft)	19.3
Depth (ft)	8.7
GRT	48.66
Engine	National
HP	160

History and Status:
1964: sold to New Zealand

111 *CHRISTINE*, PD374

Year Launched:	1948	First Owner:	W. Buchan, Fraserburgh

Principal Dimensions:	
Length (ft)	69.5
Beam (ft)	19.2
Depth (ft)	8.6
GRT	49.78
Engine	National Gas & Oil Engine Co. Ltd
HP	120

Christine.

History and Status:
1967: re-registered as SO149
1969: renamed *Golden Fort* & re-registered as D214
1977: re-registered as B204
1996: decommissioned & broken up

112 *GARLAND*, INS228

Year Launched:	1949	First Owner:	J. More, Hopeman

Principal Dimensions:	
Length (ft)	53.2
Beam (ft)	16.1
Depth (ft)	78.0
GRT	30.33
Engine	
HP	

Garland, INS228, in Whitby.

History and Status:
1971: sold to Hartlepool
1989: ceased fishing & later broken up

113 *OCEAN HARVEST*, FR279

Year Launched:	1949	First Owner:	W. Summers, Fraserburgh

Principal Dimensions:	
Length (ft)	72.0
Beam (ft)	19.7
Depth (ft)	8.7
GRT	51.49
Engine	Gardner
HP	152

Ocean Harvest, FR279.

History and Status:
1959: collided with trawler *Woods* 5.5 miles off Buchan Ness and sank. Crew rescued. Inquiry found *Ocean Harvest* to blame as helmsman had fallen asleep

114 *SINCERE*, BCK48

Year Launched:	1949	First Owner:	J. Morrison, Portgordon

Principal Dimensions:	
Length (ft)	54.0
Beam (ft)	17.2
Depth (ft)	7.7
GRT	28.79
Engine	Gardner
HP	114

Sincere, BCK48, as A555, ashore near Scarborough in 1968.

History and Status:
Re-registered as A555
1967: sold to Scarborough
1968: ran aground in thick fog just south of Cayton Bay. Crew rescued. Some equipment was salvaged but vessel was a total loss

115 *PROGRESSIVE*, SH28

Year Launched:	1949	First Owner:	J. Douglas & others, Filey

Principal Dimensions:	
Length (ft)	53.8
Beam (ft)	17.65
Depth (ft)	7.35
GRT	44.0
Engine	Gardner
HP	120

Progressive, SH28, off Scarborough. (George Westwood)

History and Status:
1986: renamed *Girl Catherine*
1995: decommissioned under 1994/95 scheme & broken up

116 *HONEYDEW*, BF307

Year Launched:	1951	First Owner:	F. West, Gardenstown

Principal Dimensions:	
Length (ft)	70.0
Beam (ft)	19.5
Depth (ft)	8.5
GRT	49.82
Engine	Gardner
HP	152

Honeydew, BF307, with steading sail up leaving Fraserburgh.

History and Status:
1963: sold to Ireland & re-registered as S39 at Skibbereen

117 *LORANTHUS*, BF317

Year Launched:	1951	First Owner:	J. Ritchie

Principal Dimensions:	
Length (ft)	70.3
Beam (ft)	19.6
Depth (ft)	8.8
GRT	49.67
Engine	Gardner
HP	152

Loranthus, BF317.

History and Status:
1960: renamed *Northern Light*, FR96
1970: renamed *Christella*
1978: renamed *Caledonia* & re-registered as PD234
1979: sank in gale 20 miles off Peterhead. Crew rescued by supply vessel *Maureen Sea*

118 *XMAS MORN*, FR124

Year Launched:	1952	First Owner:	D. Ritchie, Fraserburgh

Principal Dimensions:	
Length (ft)	70.5
Beam (ft)	19.4
Depth (ft)	8.4
GRT	48.69
Engine	Kelvin
HP	132

Xmas Morn, FR124, in 1961.

History and Status:
Sold to Ireland & re-registered as D426

119 *CORNUCOPIA*, FR319

Year Launched:	1952	First Owner:	W. Cardno, Fraserburgh

Principal Dimensions:	
Length (ft)	72.0
Beam (ft)	19.8
Depth (ft)	8.4
GRT	51.34
Engine	Gardner
HP	152

Cornucopia, FR319, leaving Fraserburgh.

History and Status:
Sold to Northern Ireland, renamed *Fidelis* & re-registered as N219

120 *BRIGHTER HOPE*, FR371

Year Launched:	1953	First Owner:	A. Watt, Fraserburgh

Principal Dimensions:	
Length (ft)	69.7
Beam (ft)	19.3
Depth (ft)	8.0
GRT	46.65
Engine	Kelvin
HP	132

History and Status:
1974: sold to Northern Ireland, renamed *Cloudless Morn* & re-registered as B176

121 *FRAGRANCE*, FR343

Year Launched:	1953	First Owner:	W. Pirie, Fraserburgh

Principal Dimensions:	
Length (ft)	32.3
Beam (ft)	40.8
Depth (ft)	4.3
GRT	6.02
Engine	Kelvin
HP	30

The small yawl *Fragrance*, FR343.

History and Status:
Re-registered as AH61, FR335
1999: ceased fishing

122 *FIDELITY*, LH390

Year Launched:	1953	First Owner:	Unknown

Principal Dimensions:	
Length (ft)	
Beam (ft)	
Depth (ft)	
GRT	
Engine	
HP	

Fidelity, LH390.

History and Status:
Details unknown, although said to be very similar to *Fragrance*

123 *GIRL PAT*, FR374

Year Launched:	1953	First Owner:	P. Summers, Fraserburgh

Principal Dimensions:	
Length (ft)	74.7
Beam (ft)	21.0
Depth (ft)	8.1
GRT	52.12
Engine	Blackstone
HP	160

Girl Pat, FR374, passing Riverside Road and Williamson's Lookout en route into Great Yarmouth.

History and Status:
1983: sold to Ireland, renamed *Utopia* & re-registered as D567
1989: ceased fishing

124 *LUSTRE*, PD379

Year Launched:	1954	First Owner:	J. Buchan, Peterhead

Principal Dimensions:	
Length (ft)	74.0
Beam (ft)	19.8
Depth (ft)	8.3
GRT	51.4
Engine	Gardner
HP	152

History and Status:
1962: sold to Northern Ireland & re-registered as N320
1989: ceased fishing

125 *LAVEROCK*, LH3

Year Launched:	1954	First Owner:	W. Liston Ltd, Newhaven

Principal Dimensions:	
Length (ft)	73.3
Beam (ft)	
Depth (ft)	
GRT	48.0
Engine	Gardner
HP	152

History and Status:
Sold to Ireland, renamed *Bridget Caroline* & re-registered as W?
1962: sold for pleasure

126 *MFV1255*

Year Launched:	1955	First Owner:	The Admiralty

Principal Dimensions:	
Length (ft)	69.2
Beam (ft)	19.8
Depth (ft)	10.0
GRT	77.0
Engine	Lister Blackstone
HP	160

History and Status:
Built as a naval auxiliary tender
1976: still in commission

127 *DAYSTAR*, INS317

| Year Launched: | 1955 | First Owner: | E. Farquhar, Lossiemouth |

Principal Dimensions:	
Length (ft)	61.1
Beam (ft)	18.2
Depth (ft)	6.6
GRT	30.97
Engine	Gardner
HP	152

History and Status:
1972: re-registered as WK84
1982: sank in Pentland Firth 12 miles from Holborn Head

128 *AZAREEL*, FR57

| Year Launched: | 1955 | First Owner: | W. Sutherland, Fraserburgh |

Principal Dimensions:	
Length (ft)	68.8
Beam (ft)	19.7
Depth (ft)	8.5
GRT	49.36
Engine	Gardner
HP	152

Azareel, FR57, in Fraserburgh harbour.

History and Status:
1994: decommissioned and broken up

129 *XMAS STAR*, FR87

Year Launched:	1955	First Owner:	A. Stephen, Fraserburgh

Principal Dimensions:	
Length (ft)	72.1
Beam (ft)	19.8
Depth (ft)	8.6
GRT	52.95
Engine	Gardner
HP	152

Xmas Star, FR87, as *Bonaventure*, FR300.

History and Status:
1977: re-registered as BF221
1980: renamed *Bonaventure* & re-registered as FR300
1985: decommissioned
1986: converted to diving boat, working from Scarborough and Oban
2000: based in Narvik & taking diving expeditions along the Norwegian coast

130 *ALLIANCE*, A95

Year Launched:	1956	First Owner:	Brebner Fishing Co. Ltd, Aberdeen

Principal Dimensions:	
Length (ft)	70.3
Beam (ft)	19.9
Depth (ft)	8.4
GRT	49.95
Engine	Kelvin
HP	132

Alliance, A95.

History and Status:
1965: sold to Hartlepool

131 *TRUE VINE*, FR186

Year Launched:	1957	First Owner:	A. Buchan, Fraserburgh

Principal Dimensions:	
Length (ft)	75.2
Beam (ft)	20.7
Depth (ft)	8.9
GRT	58.12
Engine	Gardner
HP	152

True Vine, FR186.

History and Status:
1967: renamed *Golden Promise* & re-registered as PD103
1977: renamed *Lynmarie*
1979: renamed *White Heather*
1981: renamed *Amorilla* & re-registered FR405
1983: sold to Northern Ireland & re-registered as N216

132 *WATCHFUL*, BF107

Year Launched:	1958	First Owner:	J. Reid, Gardenstown

Principal Dimensions:	
Length (ft)	60
Beam (ft)	19.2
Depth (ft)	7.8
GRT	36.73
Engine	Gardner
HP	114

Wilson's last boat, *Watchful*, BF107.

History and Status:
1991: renamed *Pleiades* & re-registered as BF155
1996: decommissioned and broken up at Fraserburgh

6

Yard Lists for Fishing Vessels by James Noble & Co.

1 *WISTARIA*, BCK116

Year Launched:	1932	First Owner:	J. Flett, Findochty

Principal Dimensions:	
Length (ft)	40.2
Beam (ft)	13.6
Depth (ft)	4.6
GRT	11.32
Engine	
HP	

History and Status:
1938: sold to Fleetwood

2 *FLORENTINE*, CN197

Year Launched:	1932	First Owner:	Walter MacConnachie, Carradale

Principal Dimensions:	
Length (ft)	48.3
Beam (ft)	4.6
Depth (ft)	6.3
GRT	18.58
Engine	Kelvin
HP	44

Florentine lying alongside at Fraserburgh, soon after her launch. (Lachie Paterson)

History and Status:
1959: re-registered as W197
1965: re-registered as OB122
1967: re-registered as SY27
1967: re-registered as TT92
1971: renamed *Misty Morn* & re-registered as CY41, owned by the late Lachie Morrison, lobster fisherman, of Grimsay
1991: ceased fishing

3 *CLUARAN*, CN240

Year Launched:	1932	First Owner:	W. Galbraith, Carradale

Principal Dimensions:	
Length (ft)	48.5
Beam (ft)	14.6
Depth (ft)	6.4
GRT	20.39
Engine	Kelvin
HP	44

Cluaran moored up at Waterfoot.

History and Status:
1948: re-registered as BK149, CK100, P283
1969: re-registered as BN9
1974: re-registered as UL168
1986: re-registered as DO62
1998: broken up

4 *ALBAN*, CN242

Year Launched:	1932	First Owner:	R. Galbraith, Carradale

Principal Dimensions:	
Length (ft)	48.3
Beam (ft)	14.6
Depth (ft)	6.5
GRT	20.63
Engine	Kevin
HP	44

Alban, as WK222.

History and Status:
1947: re-registered as WK222
1984: broken up at Scrabster

5 *AMY HARRIS*, CN249

Year Launched:	1932	First Owner:	A. Galbraith, Carradale

Principal Dimensions:	
Length (ft)	48.0
Beam (ft)	14.6
Depth (ft)	6.5
GRT	20.0
Engine	Kelvin
HP	44

Amy Harris, CN249, having a scrub.
(Lachie Paterson)

History and Status:
1959: sold to England

6 *ENTERPRISE*, CN256

Year Launched:	1933	First Owner:	A. Cook, Campbeltown

Principal Dimensions:	
Length (ft)	49.4
Beam (ft)	15.8
Depth (ft)	5.8
GRT	20.95
Engine	Kelvin
HP	66

Enterprise under construction.

History and Status:
Re-registered as SY96
1964: re-registered as WK319
Sold to Northern Ireland & re-registered as B629

7 *MAIRI BHAN*, CN259

Year Launched:	1933	First Owner:	J. Galbraith, Carradale

Principal Dimensions:	
Length (ft)	48.5
Beam (ft)	15.0
Depth (ft)	6.4
GRT	20.95
Engine	Kelvin
HP	88

Mairi Bhan alongside at North Bay.
(Lachie Paterson)

History and Status:
1952: re-registered as WK176
1961: re-registered as PT8
Later sold to Burtonport

8 *MOIRA*, CN261

Year Launched:	1933	First Owner:	C. Spiers, Campbeltown

Principal Dimensions:	
Length (ft)	48.2
Beam (ft)	15.5
Depth (ft)	6.3
GRT	20.5
Engine	Kelvin
HP	66

History and Status:
1946: sold to Ministry of War Transport

9 *SILVER CLOUD*, CN267

Year Launched:	1933	First Owner:	C. Campbell, Carradale

Principal Dimensions:	
Length (ft)	49.2
Beam (ft)	15.0
Depth (ft)	6.3
GRT	20.92
Engine	Kelvin
HP	66

Silver Cloud alongside at Noss Head. (Lachie Paterson)

History and Status:
1946: sold to Ministry of War Transport

10 *MILKY WAY*, FR374

Year Launched:	1933	First Owner:	G. Summers, Fraserburgh

Principal Dimensions:	
Length (ft)	49.7
Beam (ft)	16.5
Depth (ft)	7.6
GRT	28.05
Engine	Kelvin
HP	44

Milky Way after being sold to Berwick.

History and Status:
1936: re-registered as BK136
1968: re-registered as LK106
2001: ceased fishing
2007: unknown owners, La Gomera, Canary Islands

11 *OCEAN PEARL*, FR378

Year Launched:	1933	First Owner:	G. Noble, Fraserburgh

Principal Dimensions:	
Length (ft)	39.9
Beam (ft)	13.9
Depth (ft)	6.7
GRT	16.72
Engine	Paxman
HP	30

Ocean Pearl as PD393.

History and Status:
1939: requisitioned by the Admiralty
1945: re-registered as A333
1948: re-registered as PD393
1968: sold for pleasure at Whitby
1981: moved to Staines, Middlesex
1997: moved to Combes boatyard, Emsworth
1999: restored by Nick Gates and currently sailing

12 *QUEEN OF THE FLEET*, CN269

Year Launched:	1933	First Owner:	D. Campbeltown, Campbeltown

Principal Dimensions:	
Length (ft)	48.7
Beam (ft)	15.0
Depth (ft)	6.5
GRT	21.81
Engine	Kelvin
HP	66

Queen of the Fleet, CN269, at Waterfoot.

History and Status:
1966: sold to Suffolk

13 *SINCERITY*, AH39

Year Launched:	1933	First Owner:	H. Smith, Arbroath

Principal Dimensions:	
Length (ft)	39.6
Beam (ft)	13.6
Depth (ft)	6.1
GRT	14.78
Engine	Kelvin
HP	44

Sincerity, AH39, ashore after vandals had let go her ropes and she had drifted onto the slip.

History and Status:
1973: sold to England

14 *MONSOON*, BA265

Year Launched:	1933	First Owner:	Unknown

Principal Dimensions:	
Length (ft)	45.8
Beam (ft)	14.2
Depth (ft)	5.6
GRT	16.0
Engine	Gleniffer
HP	80

History and Status:
1948: re-registered as TT132
1953: sold and converted to cargo carrier

15 *SUSTAINER*, INS273

Year Launched:	1933	First Owner:	J. Main, Hopeman

Principal Dimensions:	
Length (ft)	
Beam (ft)	
Depth (ft)	
GRT	
Engine	
HP	

Sustainer, INS273, the inside boat alongside.

History and Status:
No known details

16 *INCENTIVE*, BA18

Year Launched:	1934	First Owner:	W. McKenzie, Girvan

Principal Dimensions:	
Length (ft)	47.0
Beam (ft)	15.0
Depth (ft)	5.7
GRT	17.97
Engine	Gleniffer
HP	80

History and Status:
1964: re-registered as KY158 & renamed *Akela*
1977: sold to Holland

17 *SEAFLOWER*, FR47

Year Launched:	1934	First Owner:	J. Noble, Fraserburgh

Principal Dimensions:	
Length (ft)	60.5
Beam (ft)	17.2
Depth (ft)	7.4
GRT	34.65
Engine	Kelvin
HP	88

History and Status:
Re-registered as SY161
1958: sunk off Broad Bay, Lewis

18 *HARMONY*, INS4

Year Launched:	1934	First Owner:	W. McPherson, Hopeman

Principal Dimensions:	
Length (ft)	50.9
Beam (ft)	15.2
Depth (ft)	6.8
GRT	23.67
Engine	Kelvin
HP	66

Harmony as SY212 in the 1950s.

History and Status:
Re-registered as SY212, TT46
1964: sold to Fleetwood

19 *ACHIEVE*, INS47

Year Launched:	1934	First Owner:	C. More, Hopeman

Principal Dimensions:	
Length (ft)	53.6
Beam (ft)	16.4
Depth (ft)	6.6
GRT	24.5
Engine	Gardner
HP	102

History and Status:
1955: re-registered as BF20
1958: sold to Northern Ireland & re-registered as N120

20 *WATERCRESS*, CN3

Year Launched:	1934	First Owner:	R. McDougal, Carradale

Principal Dimensions:	
Length (ft)	49.8
Beam (ft)	15.3
Depth (ft)	5.7
GRT	19.54
Engine	Kelvin
HP	66

Watercress, CN3, at Waterfoot, Carradale.

History and Status:
1964: ceased fishing

21 *SILVER CREST*, BA61

Year Launched:	1934	First Owner:	J. McCrindle, Girvan

Principal Dimensions:	
Length (ft)	48.0
Beam (ft)	15.0
Depth (ft)	6.4
GRT	20.74
Engine	Gleniffer
HP	80

History and Status:
1947: re-registered as CN76
1950: re-registered as TT75
1986: sold for pleasure
2010: derelict at Drumnadrochit, Loch Ness, and later sank

22 *SHEEMAUN*

NAVAL ARCHITECTS. **G. L. WATSON & CO.** YACHT BROKERS.
147, BLYTHSWOOD STREET, GLASGOW.

FOR SALE

48 Tons Twin-Screw Motor Yacht.
For sale, owner having bought larger vessel. Dimensions: 60ft. × 12.7ft.; 6ft. draft. Built 1924 by Brooke, Lowestoft. Pitch pine hull, teak deck. Copper fastened. Two 45 h.p. Gleniffer paraffin engines, new 1929. Speed 9 knots. Brooke electric lighting set. Two boats, new. First-class condition throughout.

18ft. Y.R.A. National Class Boat.
Built by Wm. Fife & Son in 1933. Excellent condition.

Auxiliary Ketch about 90 Tons Y.M.
Designed by W. Fife & Son and built by them in 1929 to Lloyd's special survey. An excellent vessel with very complete inventory.

60 Tons Aux. Berm. Ketch
"BERENICE"
(LYING FITTED OUT AT BRIXHAM).
Built 1923 to Lloyd's 15 A 1 class. Splendid condition and accommodation. Just passed through Lloyd's survey. A purchaser could have instant delivery.
Also: 6-metre yacht built 1926. Lying in store at Brixham. Both above yachts are under the care of Captain G. Dalley, The Gables, Furseham, Brixham.

300 Tons Auxiliary Schooner.
This excellent vessel is for sale at an attractive price. She was built in excess of Lloyd's requirements to our design and under our supervision. She is an especially high-class yacht, well adapted for ocean cruising and her inventory is completely comprehensive. She went through Lloyd's survey in May. Immediate delivery could be given.

NEW YACHT FOR SALE

25 Tons Twin-Screw Motor Yacht.
Built this year to our design and under our supervision. Dimensions:—Length O.A., 45ft.; breadth, 12.5ft.; draft, 4.8ft. Two Parsons 4-cylinder paraffin motors, 20/25 h.p. each. A strongly constructed and able seaboat. Fully fitted out, and immediate delivery could be given.

An article from the 1930s.

Year Launched:	1935	First Owner:	Ernest Richards, Matlock

Principal Dimensions:	
Length (ft)	42.4
Beam (ft)	12.5
Depth (ft)	7.5
GRT	22.0
Engine	(1957) 2 × Parsons petrol/paraffin
HP	2 × 27

History and Status:
Gentlemen's Motor Yacht designed by G.L. Watson
1935: sold to L.S. Saunders
1936: sold to Harold Bell
1930: sold to Roy Calvert-Link
1945: Naval Department of Sea Transport
1950–1965: various owners
1967: sold to Rear Admiral G.T.S. Gray, Midhurst, Sussex. Reg. Littlehampton. Home port Chichester
1981: sold to Ian Pearson
1987: sold to Dr Rodney Pell and still sailing

23 *UBEROUS*, FR188

Year Launched:	1935	First Owner:	G. Duthie, Fraserburgh

Principal Dimensions:	
Length (ft)	57.5
Beam (ft)	17.9
Depth (ft)	7.1
GRT	29.74
Engine	Gardner
HP	102

History and Status:
Re-registered as BK34
1972: converted for pleasure with a ketch rig

24 *ALERT*, BF234

Year Launched:	1935	First Owner:	W. Cowie, Macduff

Principal Dimensions:	
Length (ft)	50.6
Beam (ft)	16.3
Depth (ft)	6.3
GRT	24.0
Engine	Kelvin
HP	88

Alert, BF234.

History and Status:
1952: re-registered as WK194
1959: re-registered as LK467
1979: ceased fishing and derelict at Charlestown

25 *HALCYON*, WK194

Year Launched:	1935	First Owner:	J. Duncan, Wick

Principal Dimensions:	
Length (ft)	52.3
Beam (ft)	16.3
Depth (ft)	6.3
GRT	24.1
Engine	Kelvin
HP	88

Halcyon, WK194.

History and Status:
Re-registered as LK467
1979: ceased fishing

26 *GLEANER*, BF238

Year Launched:	1935	First Owner:	W. Joiner, Whitehills

Principal Dimensions:	
Length (ft)	40.0
Beam (ft)	13.5
Depth (ft)	5.6
GRT	13.75
Engine	Kelvin
HP	44

Gleaner lying half submerged alongside Macduff harbour wall.

History and Status:
1963: wrecked off Macduff

27 *WESTWARD*

Year Launched:	1935	First Owner:	Built for pleasure

Principal Dimensions:	
Length (ft)	39.2
Beam (ft)	13.6
Depth (ft)	5.8
GRT	17.07
Engine	Kelvin
HP	66

History and Status:
1941: first registered as PD295
1943: re-registered as A557, BA168, GK164
Renamed *Happy Return*, re-registered as ME149, UL164
1987: re-registered as WK130
2007: ceased fishing and owned in Cornwall
2016: broken up at Galmpton

28 *OAK LEA*, BCK51

Year Launched:	1936	First Owner:	J. Wilson, Buckie

Principal Dimensions:	
Length (ft)	50.9
Beam (ft)	16.1
Depth (ft)	6.5
GRT	20.96
Engine	Kelvin
HP	88

Oak Lea, TT131, at Mallaig.

History and Status:
1947: re-registered as TT131
1961: re-registered as OB74, based in Tobermory
1986: registry cancelled
2000: vessel reported ashore at Balmacara and subsequently transported to a farm at Kirkton, where she was later chopped up and burnt

29 *LILY OAK*, BCK94

Year Launched:	1936	First Owner:	A. Wilson, Buckie

Principal Dimensions:	
Length (ft)	50.0
Beam (ft)	15.6
Depth (ft)	6.6
GRT	23.17
Engine	Kelvin
HP	88

History and Status:
1950: re-registered as CN131
1956: renamed *Freedom* & re-registered as LH49, LK520
1962: sold to London

30 *VENUS STAR*, FR223

Year Launched:	1936	First Owner:	T. Summers, Fraserburgh

Principal Dimensions:	
Length (ft)	58.8
Beam (ft)	17.8
Depth (ft)	8.3
GRT	30.09
Engine	Kelvin
HP	88

Venus Star, FR223, in Fraserburgh harbour.

History and Status:
Re-registered as INS189
1957: caught fire and sank

31 *CONCORD*, BA112

Year Launched:	1936	First Owner:	P. Murray, Buckie

Principal Dimensions:	
Length (ft)	48.0
Beam (ft)	15.0
Depth (ft)	5.8
GRT	19.39
Engine	Kelvin
HP	66

A drawing by unknown artist of *Concord*, BA112, as BCK21. (Buckie & District Fishing Heritage Centre)

History and Status:
1939: re-registered as BCK21
1946: renamed *Dreadnought* & re-registered as LH144
1956: re-registered as PL2
1960: sold to Portavogie

32 *MARION*, BA170

Year Launched:	1936	First Owner:	W. McCreath, Girvan

Principal Dimensions:	
Length (ft)	48.0
Beam (ft)	15.0
Depth (ft)	6.3
GRT	20.41
Engine	
HP	

History and Status:
Re-registered as SY242
1969: re-registered as CK124
1979: converted for pleasure

33 *MANORA*, BA180

Year Launched:	1937	First Owner:	R. Greig, Girvan

Principal Dimensions:	
Length (ft)	48.0
Beam (ft)	15.0
Depth (ft)	6.3
GRT	20.41
Engine	
HP	

History and Status:
Sunk during Second World War

34 *MINICOY*, BA224

Year Launched:	1937	First Owner:	R. Greig, Girvan

Principal Dimensions:	
Length (ft)	49.3
Beam (ft)	15.0
Depth (ft)	6.0
GRT	19.97
Engine	
HP	

Minicoy coming into Girvan. (Lachie Paterson)

History and Status:
BA33 at some time
1940: requisitioned by the Admiralty as harbour ferry
1941: hit a mine off St Ann's Head, at entrance to Milford Haven. Crew of three lost

35 *VIOLA*, BF370

Year Launched:	1937	First Owner:	J. West, Fraserburgh

Principal Dimensions:	
Length (ft)	645.0
Beam (ft)	18.8
Depth (ft)	8.5
GRT	42.57
Engine	National
HP	150

Viola underway.

History and Status:
Re-registered BCK31

36 *BLOOM*, FR336

Year Launched:	1937	First Owner:	A. Noble, Fraserburgh

Principal Dimensions:	
Length (ft)	60.0
Beam (ft)	17.9
Depth (ft)	8.2
GRT	39.63
Engine	Gardner
HP	102

Bloom, FR336, leaving Fraserburgh.

History and Status:
1957: sank on the west coast

37 *SEAFARER*, BA294

Year Launched:	1938	First Owner:	R. McCrindle, Maidens

Principal Dimensions:	
Length (ft)	50.2
Beam (ft)	15.6
Depth (ft)	5.5
GRT	19.81
Engine	
HP	

Seafarer as LT448 *c*.1970.

History and Status:
1947: re-registered as CN177, WA15
1969: re-registered as LT448
1979: re-registered as FY417
1983: ceased fishing

38 *CRAIGIELEA*, BF447

Year Launched:	1938	First Owner:	R. Thomson, Macduff

Principal Dimensions:	
Length (ft)	39.8
Beam (ft)	13.8
Depth (ft)	6.0
GRT	14.83
Engine	Gardner
HP	48

Craigielea alongside at Macduff.

History and Status:
Re-registered as AH90
Renamed *Christmas Rose* & re-registered as BF366
1977/78: sold to Workington/Maryport
1994: decommissioned at Whitehaven

39 *LLOYD GEORGE*, FR417

Year Launched:	1938	First Owner:	R. Stephen, Fraserburgh

Principal Dimensions:	
Length (ft)	31.0
Beam (ft)	11.0
Depth (ft)	5.0
GRT	7.55
Engine	Kelvin
HP	15

History and Status:
Re-registered as BCK20
Renamed *Concord 2* & re-registered as CY136

40 *BUDDING ROSE*, INS356

Year Launched:	1938	First Owner:	Unknown

Principal Dimensions:	
Length (ft)	
Beam (ft)	
Depth (ft)	
GRT	
Engine	
HP	

History and Status:
No known details

41 *BELLA BUCHAN*, FR151

Year Launched:	1939	First Owner:	R. Buchan, Cairnbulg

Principal Dimensions:	
Length (ft)	25.0
Beam (ft)	9.5
Depth (ft)	3.5
GRT	3.74
Engine	Kelvin
HP	15

History and Status:
Renamed *Ebenezer*, BCK28
1961: renamed *Snowflake* & re-registered as PD369
1967: renamed *Thistle*

42 *MARGARET ANN 2*, OB49

Year Launched:	1939	First Owner:	J. Manson, Mallaig

Principal Dimensions:	
Length (ft)	49.4
Beam (ft)	15.8
Depth (ft)	5.8
GRT	20.95
Engine	Kelvin
HP	66

Margaret Ann 2, OB49, as *Enterprise*, WK319, in Helmsdale.

History and Status:
1949: re-registered as TT16
1954: renamed *Enterprise* & re-registered as KY56, SY296
1964: re-registered as WK319
1967: re-registered as B629
Later sold to Wexford & re-registered as WD125

43 *BOY'S OWN*, FR395

Year Launched:	1939	First Owner:	G. Duthie, Fraserburgh

Principal Dimensions:	
Length (ft)	24.7
Beam (ft)	9.1
Depth (ft)	4.3
GRT	4.35
Engine	Kelvin
HP	15

History and Status:
Renamed *Fruitful* & re-registered as BCK176

44 *ERICA*, BA20

Year Launched:	1939	First Owner:	J. McCreath, Girvan

Principal Dimensions:	
Length (ft)	49.0
Beam (ft)	15.0
Depth (ft)	5.8
GRT	19.79
Engine	Kelvin
HP	66

History and Status:
1960: renamed *Summer Rose* & re-registered as LH220
1969: re-registered as LK671
1986: decommissioned

45 *MARIE*, BA50

Year Launched:	1939	First Owner:	H. Anderson, Dunure

Principal Dimensions:	
Length (ft)	52.0
Beam (ft)	16.0
Depth (ft)	7.1
GRT	27.41
Engine	Gardner
HP	85

Marie, BA50, at Dunure.

History and Status:
Re-registered as W150, CN160
1977: ceased fishing and sold for pleasure

46 *QUIET WATERS*, PD20

Year Launched:	1939	First Owner:	T. Stephen, Peterhead

Principal Dimensions:	
Length (ft)	58.0
Beam (ft)	18.0
Depth (ft)	8.2
GRT	38.52
Engine	Kelvin
HP	132

Quiet Waters, PD20, passing the old lifeboat station and ramp at Peterhead.

History and Status:
1949: re-registered as WK12
1957: renamed *Harvest Moon* & re-registered as N65
1977: re-registered as DO50
1979: re-registered as G153

47 *AVAIL*, BA107

Year Launched:	1940	First Owner:	J. McCreath, Girvan

Principal Dimensions:	
Length (ft)	50.0
Beam (ft)	15.0
Depth (ft)	6.4
GRT	24.63
Engine	Kelvin
HP	88

History and Status:
Re-registered as LH23
1969: re-registered as AH122
1995: broken up at Methil

48 *CARRICK LASS*, BA109

Year Launched:	1940	First Owner:	R. Greig, Girvan

Principal Dimensions:	
Length (ft)	50.0
Beam (ft)	15.0
Depth (ft)	6.4
GRT	24.63
Engine	Kelvin
HP	88

Carrick Lass, BA109, at Portpatrick.

History and Status:
1969: re-registered as RX167
1971: re-registered as LT136
1973: re-registered as SN90

49 *BERYL*, BCK131

Year Launched:	1940	First Owner:	J. Murray, Buckie

Principal Dimensions:	
Length (ft)	59.8
Beam (ft)	17.9
Depth (ft)	8.3
GRT	40.77
Engine	Kelvin
HP	88

Beryl, BCK131.

History and Status:
1960: sunk east of Aberdeen after collision with a cargo vessel

50 *FLORA FRASER*, FR181

Year Launched:	1940	First Owner:	J. Ritchie, Fraserburgh

Principal Dimensions:	
Length (ft)	66.0
Beam (ft)	17.6
Depth (ft)	9.3
GRT	40.95
Engine	Kelvin
HP	132

History and Status:
Renamed *Be Ready*
1952: renamed *Gowanhill* & re-registered as PD262
1958: sunk

ADMIRALTY MOTOR FISHING VESSELS

Typical Admiralty 50ft MFV.

Principal Dimensions:	
Length (ft)	98.0
Beam (ft)	15.2
Depth (ft)	3.5
Engine	Atlantic
HP	60

51	MFV673 (1940)	(renamed *Josephine* at Plymouth & converted to pleasure)
52	MFV674 (1941)	(renamed *Inveraray Castle* & registered as BM83)
53	MFV946 (1941)	(sold to Ceylon, 1946)
54	MFV947 (1941)	(sold to Royal Indian Navy, 1946)
55	MFV948 (1941)	(renamed *Viking* & registered as SY150)
56	MFV949	(vessel ordered, then cancelled and not built)

Principal Dimensions:	
Length (ft)	75.5
Beam (ft)	19.8
Depth (ft)	5.5
Engine	Lister Blackstone
HP	160

57	MFV1001 (1941)	(renamed *Resurgam* & registered as LT139)
58	MFV1002 (1941)	(renamed *Anthony Stevenson* & registered as PZ331)
59	MFV1003 (1942)	(renamed *Pre-Eminent* & registered as FR247)
60	MFV1053 (1943)	(renamed *W & S* & registered as PZ193)
61	MFV1079 (1943)	(renamed *Rossekop* at Gibraltar, 1972)
62	MFV1080 (1943)	(renamed *Watchful of London*, 1959)
63	MFV1091 (1943)	(renamed *Mollia* & registered as LT1234, working from Swansea)
64	MFV1092 (1944)	(sold to Hong Kong)
65	MFV1139 (1944)	(renamed *Nuts* at Ramsgate, 1959, then sold to France & renamed *Frederr* and later *Arthropode*)
66	MFV1140 (1944)	(sold to Singapore, 1947)
67	MFV1141 (1944)	(sold to Cochin, 1946)
68	MFV1142 (1945)	(renamed *Grace Dixon* at Liverpool)
69	MFV1189 (1945)	(renamed *Banshee 2*)
70	MFV1190 (1945)	(vessel still in service at Greenock in 1975)
71	MFV1213 (1945)	(renamed *Muirneag 2* & registered as SY704)

Typical Admiralty 75ft MFV.

Antony Stevenson, PZ331, alongside at Newlyn.

72 *SPINDRIFT*, OB139

Year Launched:	1946	First Owner:	J. Smith, Mallaig

Principal Dimensions:	
Length (ft)	53.0
Beam (ft)	16.3
Depth (ft)	6.2
GRT	24.81
Engine	Kelvin
HP	88

Spindrift, OB139, at Scarborough.

History and Status:
1964: renamed *Ocean Starlight* & re-registered as BF334
1968: re-registered as BCK238
1977: re-registered as DO31
1977: sold to Sligo & re-registered as SO706
1994: ceased fishing

73 *BOY JAMES*, BCK8

Year Launched:	1946	First Owner:	W. Campbell, Findochty

Principal Dimensions:	
Length (ft)	25.0
Beam (ft)	9.6
Depth (ft)	3.9
GRT	4.21
Engine	Stuart Turner
HP	12

History and Status:
1964: sold to Gourdon

74 *AFTON WATERS*, BCK97

Year Launched:	1946	First Owner:	J. Murray, Buckie

Principal Dimensions:	
Length (ft)	53.1
Beam (ft)	16.1
Depth (ft)	6.2
GRT	24.85
Engine	Kelvin
HP	88

Afton Waters, BCK97.

History and Status:
1955: renamed *Evelyn* & re-registered as TT58
1985: decommissioned and sold to Ireland

75 *MARY MANSON 2*, OB155

Year Launched:	1946	First Owner:	J. Manson, Mallaig

Principal Dimensions:	
Length (ft)	51.5
Beam (ft)	16.3
Depth (ft)	6.9
GRT	24.89
Engine	Kelvin
HP	88

History and Status:
1959: renamed *Harvest Queen* & re-registered as BK141
1989: ceased fishing
2010: last reported sitting in Charlestown awaiting renovation

76 *PRIMROSE*, OB172

Year Launched:	1946	First Owner:	C. Duncan, Mallaig

Principal Dimensions:	
Length (ft)	51.8
Beam (ft)	16.2
Depth (ft)	6.1
GRT	23.64
Engine	Kelvin
HP	66

Primrose, OB172, alongside *Spindrift* at Scarborough.

History and Status:
1969: renamed *Elinda* & re-registered as LH447
1977: re-registered as CY138
1989: re-registered as UL87
1991: ceased fishing and converted to yacht
2019: for sale at Kip Marina

77 *ELMAR*, BA188

Year Launched:	1946	First Owner:	D. Smith, Girvan

Principal Dimensions:	
Length (ft)	51.5
Beam (ft)	16.2
Depth (ft)	6.2
GRT	24.21
Engine	Gleniffer
HP	80

Elmar, BA188, in Dunbar during her time with the Institute of Seaweed Research.

History and Status:
1954: used by Institute of Seaweed Research for seaweed testing
Renamed *Integrity*, BA188, BA160

78 *CABERFEIDH*, BRD343

Year Launched:	1946	First Owner:	K. Mckenzie, Ardneaskin

Principal Dimensions:	
Length (ft)	51.6
Beam (ft)	16.3
Depth (ft)	6.2
GRT	22.1
Engine	Kelvin
HP	88

Caberfeidh, as *Incentive*, KY343, leaving Pittenweem.

History and Status:
1965: renamed *Incentive 2* & re-registered as KY343
1986: re-registered as E329, FR169
1978: sold to Fleetwood
1992: ceased fishing

79 *CATHERINE & JOHN*, DO21

Year Launched:	1946	First Owner:	W. Swindlehurst, Douglas

Principal Dimensions:	
Length (ft)	44.75
Beam (ft)	16.2
Depth (ft)	6.2
GRT	29.03
Engine	
HP	110

Catherine & John, DO21, steaming out of Douglas. (Mike Craine)

History and Status:
1994: sold for pleasure

80 *SUNBEAM*, BCK165

Year Launched:	1947	First Owner:	W. Reid, Portgordon

Principal Dimensions:	
Length (ft)	52.0
Beam (ft)	16.4
Depth (ft)	6.5
GRT	22.29
Engine	Kelvin
HP	66

Sunbeam lying sunk before being refloated. She neighboured with *Afton Waters*.

History and Status:
1974: re-registered as TT117
1995: decommissioned and later broken up at Campbeltown

81 *SILVER BIRCH*, BF186

Year Launched:	1947	First Owner:	J. Ritchie, Whitehills

Principal Dimensions:	
Length (ft)	52.0
Beam (ft)	16.4
Depth (ft)	6.5
GRT	21.01
Engine	Kelvin
HP	88

Silver Birch, BF186, as TT151 at Tarbert.

History and Status:
1949: re-registered as TT151
1954: renamed *Ile Bhoddheach* & re-registered as CN6, based in Port Charlotte, Islay
1955: wrecked on the Post Rocks, west of Islay

82 *TRUE LOVE*, INS140

Year Launched:	1947	First Owner:	G. Jack, Avoch

Principal Dimensions:	
Length (ft)	48.3
Beam (ft)	16.4
Depth (ft)	5.3
GRT	18.89
Engine	Kelvin
HP	88

True Love, INS140, one of several JN boats for Avoch.

History and Status:
Renamed *Virgin 4* & re-registered as CY224, CN228
1969: renamed *May Queen*, & re-registered as LH429
1982: sold to England

83 *CONCORD III*, BCK78

Year Launched:	1947	First Owner:	P. Murray, Buckie

Principal Dimensions:	
Length (ft)	51.5
Beam (ft)	16.4
Depth (ft)	6.6
GRT	32.17
Engine	Gardner
HP	95

History and Status:
1959: re-registered as SD38
1967: re-registered as LH445
1974: sold to Galway, Ireland, & registered as G125

84 *MALLAIG VAIG*, OB304

Year Launched:	1947	First Owner:	Mallaig Fishing Co. Ltd

Principal Dimensions:	
Length (ft)	52.0
Beam (ft)	16.0
Depth (ft)	5.5
GRT	20.59
Engine	Gleniffer
HP	80

Mallaig Vaig, OB304, as *Lady Fatima*, CY44.

History and Status:
Renamed *Lady of Fatima* & re-registered as CY44
1969: renamed *Isabella* & re-registered as OB96
1979: renamed *Kestrel*
1985: caught fire & sunk off Soay

85 *MALLAIG MHOR*, OB315

Year Launched:	1947	First Owner:	D. Gillies, Mallaig

Principal Dimensions:	
Length (ft)	52.0
Beam (ft)	16.0
Depth (ft)	5.5
GRT	20.59
Engine	Kelvin
HP	88

History and Status:
1959: renamed *Florentine* & re-registered as CN74
1975: sold to England
1993: decommissioned and broken up at Fleetwood

86 *MAIGHDEAN BHAN*, UL120

Year Launched:	1947	First Owner:	J. McKenzie, Gairloch

Principal Dimensions:	
Length (ft)	46.5
Beam (ft)	16.3
Depth (ft)	6.6
GRT	23.49
Engine	Gleniffer
HP	80

History and Status:
Renamed *Diadem* & re-registered B183
1972: sold for pleasure & renamed *Lisanya*

87 *SAINT MAUGHOLD*, DO24

Year Launched:	1947	First Owner:	G. Devereau, Douglas

Principal Dimensions:	
Length (ft)	45.75
Beam (ft)	16.2
Depth (ft)	6.2
GRT	26.53
Engine	
HP	

Saint Maughold, DO24, off Peel.
(Mike Craine)

History and Status:
1989: decommissioned and sold for pleasure

88 *MAPLE LEAF*, INS131

Year Launched:	1947	First Owner:	D. Ralph, Hopeman

Principal Dimensions:	
Length (ft)	56.9
Beam (ft)	17.3
Depth (ft)	6.3
GRT	25.45
Engine	Gardner
HP	114

History and Status:
1975: ceased fishing

89 *MAID OF ERIN*, CT116

Year Launched:	1947	First Owner:	Manxmaid Fishing Co. Ltd, Port Erin

Principal Dimensions:	
Length (ft)	49.6
Beam (ft)	16.2
Depth (ft)	6.55
GRT	26.42
Engine	Gardner
HP	114

History and Status:
Scrapped in Islay

90 *CONSTANCE*, UL265

Year Launched:	1948	First Owner:	R. McKenzie, Port Henderson

Principal Dimensions:	
Length (ft)	52
Beam (ft)	16.3
Depth (ft)	6.7
GRT	23.34
Engine	Gleniffer
HP	80

Constance, UL265, as SY5.

History and Status:
Re-registered as SY5
1972: ran aground and sank off Farne Islands, Northumberland (11 September)

91 *MAIGHDEAN MHARA*, UL276

Year Launched:	1948	First Owner:	D. McKenzie, Gairloch

Principal Dimensions:	
Length (ft)	50.0
Beam (ft)	16.3
Depth (ft)	6.7
GRT	22.85
Engine	Gleniffer
HP	80

Maighdean Mhara, UL276, at Gairloch.

History and Status:
Renamed *Maggie Maclean* & re-registered as OB30
1967: renamed *Heatherbelle* & re-registered as BK213
1969: re-registered as LK263
1977: sold to Hartlepool

92 *YOUNG DAWN*, LK507

Year Launched:	1948	First Owner:	S. Cumming, Lerwick

Principal Dimensions:	
Length (ft)	51.4
Beam (ft)	
Depth (ft)	
GRT	22.08
Engine	Gardner
HP	95

Young Dawn, LK507.

History and Status:
1953: went ashore at Vementry, Shetland, drifted off and eventually sank off Pappa Little (December)

93 *GOODWILL*, LH255

Year Launched:	1948	First Owner:	A. Brown, Fisherrow

Principal Dimensions:	
Length (ft)	50.0
Beam (ft)	16.3
Depth (ft)	6.2
GRT	22.75
Engine	Gardner
HP	95

History and Status:
Re-registered as SY116
1974: re-registered as CN100
1975: sold to Fowey

94 *XMAS STAR*, INS218

Year Launched:	1948	First Owner:	J. More, Burghead

Principal Dimensions:	
Length (ft)	54.0
Beam (ft)	16.4
Depth (ft)	6.7
GRT	24.87
Engine	Gardner
HP	95

Xmas Star,
INS218.

History and Status:
Re-registered as BK103
Renamed *Summer Rose* & re-registered as LH440, WY234

95 *DAINTY LADY*, H509

Year Launched:	1948	First Owner:	T. Cowling, Bridlington

Principal Dimensions:	
Length (ft)	54.0
Beam (ft)	16.5
Depth (ft)	6.8
GRT	31.0
Engine	Gardner
HP	95

History and Status:
1977: re-registered as DO57, M507
1989: ceased fishing

96 *GUIDING STAR*, BF206

Year Launched:	1948	First Owner:	W. Levenie, Whitehills

Principal Dimensions:	
Length (ft)	49.1
Beam (ft)	16.3
Depth (ft)	6.7
GRT	24.12
Engine	Kelvin
HP	66

Guiding Star, BF206.

History and Status:
1981: re-registered as BH205
1983: re-registered as K551
1987: sold for pleasure & converted
2011: based in Oban

97 *LIBERTY*, H580

Year Launched:	1948	First Owner:	J. Sanderson, Bridlington

Principal Dimensions:	
Length (ft)	46.7
Beam (ft)	17.05
Depth (ft)	6.6
GRT	24.98
Engine	Kelvin
HP	88

History and Status:
Used for all manner of fishing: long-lining in winter, potting, fog-line fishing out of Grimsby, herring drifting out off Scarborough. Twenty years same owner until replaced by *Ocean Reward*
1977: sunk after running aground on Belhaven Sands. Cut up and Gardner 6LX removed through hole cut in side of vessel

98 *MINICOY*, BA74

Year Launched:	1948	First Owner:	J. McCrindle, Girvan

Principal Dimensions:	
Length (ft)	56.0
Beam (ft)	17.9
Depth (ft)	6.5
GRT	28.6
Engine	Gleniffer
HP	120

History and Status:
Renamed *Sapphire*
1967: renamed *Heritage*
1971: re-registered as LH462
1974: sold to England

99 *MAY LILY*, BF225

Year Launched:	1948	First Owner:	G. West, Gardenstown

Principal Dimensions:	
Length (ft)	70.0
Beam (ft)	18.8
Depth (ft)	8.8
GRT	48.39
Engine	Gardner
HP	152

May Lily, BF225.

History and Status:
1976: based in Orkney
1989: ceased fishing

100 *MALLAIG CRUACH*, OB326

Year Launched:	1948	First Owner:	Mallaig Fishing Co. Ltd

Principal Dimensions:	
Length (ft)	52.0
Beam (ft)	16.5
Depth (ft)	6.6
GRT	23.28
Engine	Gleniffer
HP	80

Mallaig Cruach as *Shining Light*, SO671.

History and Status:
1960: renamed *Scalpay Isle* & re-registered as SY429, B176
1973: renamed *Shining Light* & re-registered as B113, SO671
1990: re-registered as B671
1995: decommissioned & broken up

101 *MARGUERITE*, INS261

Year Launched:	1949	First Owner:	D. McLeman

Principal Dimensions:	
Length (ft)	53.0
Beam (ft)	16.6
Depth (ft)	6.6
GRT	24.01
Engine	
HP	

Marguerite, INS261, passing Macduff.

History and Status:
1963: sunk

102 *WHITE ROSE*, BCK39

Year Launched:	1949	First Owner:	G. Smith

Principal Dimensions:	
Length (ft)	49.3
Beam (ft)	16.5
Depth (ft)	6.7
GRT	24.53
Engine	Gleniffer
HP	80

White Rose, BCK39, at Conway.

History and Status:
1965: re-registered as PL18
1968: re-registered as TT100
1970: renamed *New Venture* & re-registered PL28
1984: laid up in Ramsey & broken up a year or two later

103 *MYRTLE*, FR9

Year Launched:	1949	First Owner:	A. Buchan, Fraserburgh

Principal Dimensions:	
Length (ft)	32.9
Beam (ft)	12.0
Depth (ft)	5.0
GRT	8.88
Engine	Kelvin
HP	33

Myrtle. (George Westwood)

History and Status:
Unknown

104 *GUIDE ME*, INS254

Year Launched:	1949	First Owner:	L. Patience, Avoch

Principal Dimensions:	
Length (ft)	49.3
Beam (ft)	17.2
Depth (ft)	6.5
GRT	24.8
Engine	Kelvin
HP	88

Guide Me, INS254.

History and Status:
Re-registered as FR3
1969: sold to Scarborough

105 *MARIGOLD*, INS256

Year Launched:	1949	First Owner:	D. Patience, Avoch

Principal Dimensions:	
Length (ft)	49.0
Beam (ft)	16.5
Depth (ft)	6.5
GRT	23.65
Engine	Kelvin
HP	88

Marigold, INS256, along with *Guide Me* being Avoch-owned.

History and Status:
Re-registered as AH50
1987: sold to Cornwall
1994: decommissioned & broken up

106 *ROSEHAUGH*, INS246

Year Launched:	1949	First Owner:	G. Jack, Avoch

Principal Dimensions:	
Length (ft)	48.6
Beam (ft)	16.8
Depth (ft)	6.8
GRT	24.98
Engine	Kelvin
HP	88

History and Status:
Renamed *Girl Jean* & re-registered as LH218 (possibly renamed back to *Rosehaugh*)
1991: ceased fishing

107 *SEAFARER*, BCK58

Year Launched:	1949	First Owner:	G. Jack, Avoch

Principal Dimensions:	
Length (ft)	53.2
Beam (ft)	16.1
Depth (ft)	66
GRT	23.96
Engine	Kelvin
HP	88

I love this photo of children fishing off *Seafarer*.

History and Status:
Re-registered as SY210 based in Ullapool
1987: decommissioned

108 *SEA HARVEST*, BCK44

Year Launched:	1949	First Owner:	D. Cowie, Buckie

Principal Dimensions:	
Length (ft)	53.0
Beam (ft)	155
Depth (ft)	7.4
GRT	26.37
Engine	Kelvin
HP	88

Sea Harvest, BCK44, at Buckie.

History and Status:
Re-registered as SY7
1986: decommissioned

109 *ELIZABETH TAYLOR*, H107

Year Launched:	1950	First Owner:	Bridlington

Principal Dimensions:	
Length (ft)	54.0
Beam (ft)	
Depth (ft)	
GRT	
Engine	
HP	

Elizabeth Taylor entering Bridlington on festival day.

History and Status:
1951: sunk off Robin Hood's Bay after being holed in collision with FR fishing boat *Incentive*

110 *SEA OTTER*

Year Launched:	1950	First Owner:	Unknown

Principal Dimensions:	
Length (ft)	34.0
Beam (ft)	12.0
Depth (ft)	5.1
GRT	16.0
Engine	Kelvin
HP	33

History and Status:
Built as a yacht
1972: owned in Woodbridge, Suffolk

111 *ROSE*, INS39

Year Launched:	1950	First Owner:	A. Skinner, Avoch

Principal Dimensions:	
Length (ft)	52.4
Beam (ft)	16.4
Depth (ft)	6.6
GRT	23.87
Engine	Kelvin
HP	88

Rose, INS39.

History and Status:
1994: decommissioned

112 *PRESS ON*, LK137

Year Launched:	1950	First Owner:	J.P. Hendry, Burra

Principal Dimensions:	
Length (ft)	69.9
Beam (ft)	19.8
Depth (ft)	8.4
GRT	49.77
Engine	Gardner
HP	152

Press On, LK137.

History and Status:
Re-registered as B70
Renamed *Prospective*

113 *REPLENISH*, LK97

Year Launched:	1950	First Owner:	J. Pottinger, Hamnavoe

Principal Dimensions:	
Length (ft)	69.9
Beam (ft)	19.5
Depth (ft)	8.5
GRT	49.75
Engine	Gardner
HP	152

History and Status:
1983: scrapped

114 *ISABELLA*, SY142

Year Launched:	1950	First Owner:	D. McMillan, Lemreway

Principal Dimensions:	
Length (ft)	49.5
Beam (ft)	16.7
Depth (ft)	6.5
GRT	24.18
Engine	Kelvin
HP	88

Isabella, SY142, at Stornoway.

History and Status:
Renamed *Kenroy*
1983: ceased fishing

115 *GOLDEN HIND*, CN199

Year Launched:	1950	First Owner:	D. MacDonald, Campbeltown

Principal Dimensions:	
Length (ft)	56.0
Beam (ft)	17.8
Depth (ft)	5.8
GRT	24.53
Engine	Kelvin
HP	88

Golden Hind, CN199, steaming out of Fraserburgh.

History and Status:
Re-registered as OB221
1978: ceased fishing

116 *FRAGRANCE, FR228*

Year Launched:	1951	First Owner:	Mr Noble, Fraserburgh

Principal Dimensions:	
Length (ft)	55.0
Beam (ft)	17.6
Depth (ft)	6.6
GRT	27.5
Engine	Kelvin
HP	132

Fragrance as *Coastal Star*, BF29.

History and Status:
1950(?): renamed *Rose Valley* & re-registered as INS79
1955: renamed *Coastal Star* & re-registered as BF29
1961: renamed *Courage* & re-registered as SH63
1988: re-registered as BA307
1991: ceased fishing & converted to yacht

117 *MAMORE*

Year Launched:	1951	First Owner:	Ballachulish Ferry Company

Principal Dimensions:	
Length (ft)	44.7
Beam (ft)	18.6
Depth (ft)	4.3
GRT	16.09
Engine	Gleniffer
HP	48

Mamore, built as a ferry and later went fishing.

History and Status:
Built as a ferry though later registered for fishing as UL107, fishing for herring
Sometime later laid up at the Culag bridge, Lochiver, for many years until being scrapped

118 *MAISIE*, TT83

Year Launched:	1952	First Owner:	D. Kerr, Tarbert

Principal Dimensions:	
Length (ft)	39.3
Beam (ft)	14.7
Depth (ft)	6.1
GRT	15.09
Engine	Kelvin
HP	44

Maisie, TT83.

History and Status:
1964: re-registered as CO154, PD71
Renamed *Planet* & re-registered as LK79

119 *LADY CAMPBELL*

Year Launched:	1952	First Owner:	E.D. Woodrow, Sanderstand, Surrey

Principal Dimensions:	
Length (ft)	32.0
Beam (ft)	9.5
Depth (ft)	5.1
GRT	11.0
Engine	2 × Perkins
HP	36

The yacht *Lady Campbell*.

History and Status:
Built as a motor cruiser
1972: sold to W.J. Bland, Beckenham, Kent

120 *MORAY LASS*, INS104

Year Launched:	1952	First Owner:	D. Jack, Hopeman

Principal Dimensions:	
Length (ft)	55.2
Beam (ft)	17.1
Depth (ft)	6.1
GRT	24.9
Engine	Gardner
HP	114

Moray Lass, INS104, off to the seine net.

History and Status:
Re-registered as WK176
1979: sold to Hartlepool

121 *GOLDEN PROMISE*, FR347

Year Launched:	1952	First Owner:	A. Buchan, Fraserburgh

Principal Dimensions:	
Length (ft)	72.1
Beam (ft)	19.7
Depth (ft)	9.3
GRT	56.56
Engine	Kelvin
HP	132

Golden Promise, FR347, at the East Anglian herring fishery.

History and Status:
Renamed *Sunlight* & re-registered as PD232
1963: sold to Ireland

122 *FERTILITY*, PD267

Year Launched:	1953	First Owner:	J.G. Hay, Peterhead

Principal Dimensions:	
Length (ft)	72.0
Beam (ft)	19.8
Depth (ft)	9.0
GRT	55.57
Engine	Kelvin
HP	132

History and Status:
Re-registered as B102

123 *QUIET WATERS*, PD275

Year Launched:	1953	First Owner:	R. Stephen, Peterhead

Principal Dimensions:	
Length (ft)	73.0
Beam (ft)	19.8
Depth (ft)	9.0
GRT	55.01
Engine	
HP	

History and Status:
1974: lost in the North Sea

124 *HARVESTER*, FR22

Year Launched:	1954	First Owner:	J. Noble, Fraserburgh

Principal Dimensions:	
Length (ft)	72.0
Beam (ft)	19.1
Depth (ft)	8.9
GRT	52.09
Engine	Gardner
HP	152

Harvester, FR22, in Fraserburgh harbour.

History and Status:
1966: renamed *Radiant Way*
1977: renamed *Radiant Morn* & re-registered as PD273, BF409
1989: sold to Belfast & re-registered as B409
1995: decommissioned & broken up

125 *KATHRYN*, RO113

Year Launched:	1954	First Owner:	T. Rae, Rothesay

Principal Dimensions:	
Length (ft)	39.5
Beam (ft)	14.8
Depth (ft)	6.1
GRT	15.36
Engine	Kelvin
HP	66

Kathryn coming into Ayr. (Richard Hodge)

History and Status:
Renamed *Fiona* & re-registered as BA3, PD66, CY171

126 *OCEAN VANGUARD*, BH3

Year Launched:	1954	First Owner:	T. Handyside, Blyth

Principal Dimensions:	
Length (ft)	41.7
Beam (ft)	14.8
Depth (ft)	6.4
GRT	16.86
Engine	Gardner
HP	95

Ocean Vanguard, BH3, as *Vivid*, ME106.

History and Status:
Re-registered as KY131, OB21
Re-named *Vivid* & re-registered as ME106

127 *RENOWN 2*, INS285

Year Launched:	1954	First Owner:	W. Farquher, Lossiemouth

Principal Dimensions:	
Length (ft)	62.4
Beam (ft)	18.6
Depth (ft)	8.3
GRT	40.85
Engine	Gardner
HP	114

Renown, INS285.

History and Status:
1979: sunk

128 *WELFARE*, FR379

Year Launched:	1954	First Owner:	R. Buchan, St Combs

Principal Dimensions:	
Length (ft)	72.2
Beam (ft)	19.7
Depth (ft)	8.9
GRT	15.44
Engine	Gardner
HP	152

Welfare, FR379, with launch aboard, in Orkney.

History and Status:
1979: sunk

129 *SINCERITY*, LH10

Year Launched:	1954	First Owner:	J. Croan, Newhaven

Principal Dimensions:	
Length (ft)	68.75
Beam (ft)	19.6
Depth (ft)	8.6
GRT	49.61
Engine	Gardner
HP	152

Sincerity, LH10, as *Girl Joyce*, FR366, at North Shields.

History and Status:
Renamed *Girl Joyce* & re-registered as FR366
Renamed *Ocean Venture*
1977: sunk

130 MFV1254

Year Launched:	1954	First Owner:	The Admiralty

Principal Dimensions:	
Length (ft)	69.2
Beam (ft)	19.8
Depth (ft)	10.0
GRT	77.0
Engine	
HP	160

MFV1254. (Maureen and Bruce Herd)

History and Status:
1954: built as a naval auxiliary tender for harbour work
1960: sold at Rosyth
1974: renamed *Leaholme*

131 *ROWANTREE*, INS290

Year Launched:	1955	First Owner:	G. Mcleod, Lossiemouth

Principal Dimensions:	
Length (ft)	63.5
Beam (ft)	18.4
Depth (ft)	7.8
GRT	37.98
Engine	Gardner
HP	152

History and Status:
1968: re-registered as BCK1
1974: renamed *Spindrift*, BCK1
1989: renamed *Sharona*, BCK1
1994: decommissioned & broken up at Dundee

132 *NIMROD*, LH50

Year Launched:	1955	First Owner:	J. Harkness, Port Seton

Principal Dimensions:	
Length (ft)	39.9
Beam (ft)	15.0
Depth (ft)	5.3
GRT	13.24
Engine	Kelvin
HP	66

History and Status:
Renamed *Brighter Morn* & re-registered as CN151, FR411, WK187
Renamed *Golden Isles* & re-registered as UL11
1996: sold to Kilkeel

133 *OCEAN GIFT*, PZ16

Year Launched:	1955	First Owner:	J. Pockley, Penzance

Principal Dimensions:	
Length (ft)	50.0
Beam (ft)	15.5
Depth (ft)	6.0
GRT	
Engine	
HP	99

Ocean Gift, PZ16, alongside.

History and Status:
Renamed *Bev Van Dan*, PZ16
Renamed *Ocean Gift* & converted to look like a tug in Essex

134 *HARVEST REAPER*, PD126

Year Launched:	1955	First Owner:	A. Strachan, Peterhead

Principal Dimensions:	
Length (ft)	39.5
Beam (ft)	14.7
Depth (ft)	6.2
GRT	15.42
Engine	Kelvin
HP	66

History and Status:
1977: sold to Hartlepool
1986: re-registered as PW58
1989: renamed *Sara Jean*
1997: ceased fishing

135 *TRIUMPH*, INS46

Year Launched:	1955	First Owner:	T. Murray, Hopeman

Principal Dimensions:	
Length (ft)	54.3
Beam (ft)	16.5
Depth (ft)	6.5
GRT	24.28
Engine	Kelvin
HP	114

History and Status:
Re-registered as LH189
1987: sold to England

136 *PRIMROSE*, INS291

Year Launched:	1955	First Owner:	W. MacLennan, Avoch

Principal Dimensions:	
Length (ft)	52.1
Beam (ft)	16.3
Depth (ft)	6.1
GRT	22.01
Engine	Kelvin
HP	88

History and Status:
2000: decommissioned

137 *POLARIS*, INS51

Year Launched:	1956	First Owner:	J. Crocket, Lossiemouth

Principal Dimensions:	
Length (ft)	52.9
Beam (ft)	17.7
Depth (ft)	6.4
GRT	24.93
Engine	Gardner
HP	114

Polaris, INS51.

History and Status:
1975: scrapped

138 *HISPERIAN*, PZ22

Year Launched:	1956	First Owner:	E. W. James, Penzance

Principal Dimensions:	
Length (ft)	40.0
Beam (ft)	14.9
Depth (ft)	6.3
GRT	20.82
Engine	Kelvin
HP	66

Hesperian, PZ22, at Par, Cornwall.

History and Status:
Re-registered as INS85, then sold to Grimsby

139 *PROCYON*, INS7

Year Launched:	1956	First Owner:	J. Bremner, Lossiemouth

Principal Dimensions:	
Length (ft)	66.0
Beam (ft)	18.7
Depth (ft)	8.3
GRT	42.3
Engine	Gardner
HP	152

Procyon, INS7, entering Lossiemouth on what looks like festival day.

History and Status:
1993: decommissioned

140 *CHICHESTER LASS*, PZ263

Year Launched:	1956	First Owner:	Messrs Shippam, Chichester

Principal Dimensions:	
Length (ft)	40.0
Beam (ft)	15.0
Depth (ft)	8.5
GRT	18.0
Engine	Kelvin
HP	88

Chichester Lass, PZ263, in among Cornish luggers in Customs House Quay, Falmouth.

History and Status:
Unknown

141 *CONCORD*, BCK59

Year Launched:	1957	First Owner:	P. Murray, Buckie

Principal Dimensions:	
Length (ft)	53.8
Beam (ft)	17.3
Depth (ft)	6.8
GRT	26.36
Engine	Gardner
HP	95

Concord, BCK59, alongside at Gairloch.

History and Status:
1966: re-registered as FR410
1982: renamed *Girl Ann* & re-registered as WK527
1982: lost 30 miles east of Wick

142 *STRATHYRE*, INS23

Year Launched:	1957	First Owner:	A. Souter, Lossiemouth

Principal Dimensions:	
Length (ft)	67.3
Beam (ft)	18.6
Depth (ft)	11.6
GRT	45.37
Engine	Gardner
HP	152

History and Status:
Cost £16,000 to build
1958: broke moorings in Lossiemouth harbour in a gale. Driven aground and broke up after salvage attempts failed

143 *THRIVE*, INS43

Year Launched:	1957	First Owner:	A. Smith, Lossiemouth

Principal Dimensions:	
Length (ft)	58.2
Beam (ft)	18.4
Depth (ft)	8.35
GRT	35.95
Engine	Gardner
HP	152

Thrive, INS43, alongside at Lossiemouth.

History and Status:
1993: decommissioned

144 *MARGARET JANE*, SH17

Year Launched:	1957	First Owner:	T. Mainprize, Scarborough

Principal Dimensions:	
Length (ft)	48.4
Beam (ft)	16.2
Depth (ft)	6.15
GRT	22.33
Engine	Kelvin
HP	88

Margaret Jane, SH17, one of the boats for the Mainprize family of Scarborough.

History and Status:
Renamed *Dorothy D* & re-registered as ME45
1981: sold to North Shields

145 *COEUR DE LION*, PZ74

Year Launched:	1957	First Owner:	R.H. Sampson, Penzance

Principal Dimensions:	
Length (ft)	45.0
Beam (ft)	15.5
Depth (ft)	8.8
GRT	23.0
Engine	2 × Davey-Paxman
HP	

History and Status:
Unknown

146 *KRISTIONA*, HL111

Year Launched:	1957	First Owner:	Kristiona Fishing Co. Ltd, Hartlepool

Principal Dimensions:	
Length (ft)	49.0
Beam (ft)	16.0
Depth (ft)	9.0
GRT	24.13
Engine	Gardner
HP	95

History and Status:
1993: decommissioned

147 *GIRL IRENE*, INS58

Year Launched:	1957	First Owner:	D. Stewart, Lossiemouth

Principal Dimensions:	
Length (ft)	52.8
Beam (ft)	17.3
Depth (ft)	6.5
GRT	24.9
Engine	Gardner
HP	114

Girl Irene, INS58, alongside at Lossiemouth.

History and Status:
Re-registered as CN202, BS193

148 *INVERLOSSIE*, UL106

Year Launched:	1957	First Owner:	G. McKay, Lochinver

Principal Dimensions:	
Length (ft)	64.2
Beam (ft)	18.9
Depth (ft)	8.2
GRT	42.61
Engine	Gardner
HP	152

Inverlossie, UL106.

History and Status:
Renamed *Ranger* & re-registered as K306, SO862

149 *AVONDALE*, HL112

Year Launched:	1958	First Owner:	R. Trueman, Hartlepool

Principal Dimensions:	
Length (ft)	4.0
Beam (ft)	16.0
Depth (ft)	9.0
GRT	24.11
Engine	Gardner
HP	95

Avondale, HL112, at Scarborough.

History and Status:
2002: ceased fishing & converted to pleasure at Hull
2020: based in Hull Marina

150 *FIONA FAY*, HL113

Year Launched:	1958	First Owner:	Janet Fishing Co. Ltd, Hartlepool

Principal Dimensions:	
Length (ft)	49.0
Beam (ft)	16.0
Depth (ft)	9.0
GRT	24.0
Engine	Gardner
HP	95

Fiona Fay rigged with a small sail.

History and Status:
1965: driven ashore on North Sands, Hartlepool & wrecked, all crew safe

151 *REYNARD*, BS13

Year Launched:	1958	First Owner:	T. Kershaw, Anglesey

Principal Dimensions:	
Length (ft)	44.9
Beam (ft)	15.9
Depth (ft)	6.3
GRT	20.35
Engine	Gardner
HP	76

History and Status:
Re-registered as FD132
Renamed *Golden Sheaf* & re-registered as CN367

152 *CASTLE EDEN*, HL115

Year Launched:	1958	First Owner:	Hartlepool Seiners Ltd

Principal Dimensions:	
Length (ft)	49.0
Beam (ft)	16.0
Depth (ft)	9.0
GRT	25.0
Engine	Gardner
HP	95

History and Status:
1968: caught fire & sank off Redcar, all crew rescued

153 *FIONAGHAL*, INS67

Year Launched:	1958	First Owner:	J. Mcleod, Lossiemouth

Principal Dimensions:	
Length (ft)	65.5
Beam (ft)	18.9
Depth (ft)	8.2
GRT	43.52
Engine	Gardner
HP	152

Fionaghal, INS67, alongside at Lerwick.

History and Status:
Renamed *Sunbeam* & re-registered as SN92

154 *AILSEA*, FD174

Year Launched:	1959	First Owner:	Boris Net Co. Ltd, Fleetwood

Principal Dimensions:	
Length (ft)	42.6
Beam (ft)	16.05
Depth (ft)	7.0
GRT	23.4
Engine	Gardner
HP	95

History and Status:
Re-registered as CN231
1991: sold to England

155 *STØRA K*

Year Launched:	1959	First Owner:	Fraserburgh

Principal Dimensions:	
Length (ft)	35.0
Beam (ft)	9.7
Depth (ft)	4.8
GRT	9.0
Engine	2 × Daimler–Benz
HP	42

Yacht *Støra K*. (Maureen and Bruce Herd)

History and Status:
Built as a yacht
1972: owned by H.E. Keene, Gloucester. Home port Exmouth

156 *LOCH KIRKAIG*, UL145

Year Launched:	1959	First Owner:	W. Mathieson, Lochinver

Principal Dimensions:	
Length (ft)	36.0
Beam (ft)	13.1
Depth (ft)	6.1
GRT	12.26
Engine	Gardner
HP	56

Loch Kirkaig, UL145, as *Fruitful*, PD31, at Rye, Sussex.

History and Status:
Renamed *Fruitful 2* & re-registered as PD31
1962: sold to Rye & renamed *Richard H Pepper* & re-registered as RX311

157 *ROSEBANK*, BF188

Year Launched:	1959	First Owner:	F. Watt, Aberdeen

Principal Dimensions:	
Length (ft)	72.4
Beam (ft)	21.0
Depth (ft)	10.3
GRT	67.65
Engine	Gardner
HP	152

Rosebank, BF188.

History and Status:
1963: sunk off Shetland and crew safe (24 January)

158 *M.D.B.*, FD153

Year Launched:	1960	First Owner:	R. Bond, Fleetwood

Principal Dimensions:	
Length (ft)	44.0
Beam (ft)	16.0
Depth (ft)	6.45
GRT	22.31
Engine	Gardner
HP	76

M.D.B., FD153, built for Fleetwood.

History and Status:
Renamed *Sincerity 5* & re-registered as AH133

159 *ACACIA*, BF199

Year Launched:	1960	First Owner:	B. Nicol, Gardenstown

Principal Dimensions:	
Length (ft)	60.3
Beam (ft)	19.5
Depth (ft)	8.1
GRT	39.95
Engine	Gardner
HP	114

Acacia, BF199, in Macduff.

History and Status:
1970: sold to Hartlepool
1984: sold to Portavogie & re-registered as B25
1985: sold to Helston
1988: sold to Newlyn
1995: ceased fishing

160 *BETTY*, FR68

Year Launched:	1960	First Owner:	W. Glenton, Bridlington

Principal Dimensions:	
Length (ft)	52.0
Beam (ft)	17.0
Depth (ft)	6.0
GRT	23.0
Engine	Gardner
HP	114

Betty, FR68, in Fraserburgh harbour.

History and Status:
1971: sold to Bridlington
1995: ceased fishing

161 *WELLSPRING*, FR307

Year Launched:	1960	First Owner:	T. West, Fraserburgh

Principal Dimensions:	
Length (ft)	39.75
Beam (ft)	15.0
Depth (ft)	6.2
GRT	15.69
Engine	Gardner
HP	76

Wellspring as BA377.

History and Status:
Re-registered as BA337
1974: sold to England (Cleveland)
1998: renamed *Spring Tide* & re-registered as WK688, LK714
2009: ashore on rocks called 'Spencie' on the north-east corner of Odiness Bay, Stronsay and later sunk

162 *WAVE SHEAF*, INS118

Year Launched:	1960	First Owner:	E. Thomson, Lossiemouth

Principal Dimensions:	
Length (ft)	68.2
Beam (ft)	19.6
Depth (ft)	7.9
GRT	44.87
Engine	Gardner
HP	200

History and Status:
1964: renamed *Marradale* & re-registered as BCK223
1974: sank in the Minch after hitting submerged object. Crew rescued after nine hours in life raft

163 *ASPIRE*, INS148

Year Launched:	1961	First Owner:	A. Skinner, Avoch

Principal Dimensions:	
Length (ft)	55.0
Beam (ft)	17.5
Depth (ft)	6.2
GRT	24.8
Engine	Gardner
HP	150

Aspire, INS148. (Peter Drummond)

History and Status:
2007: off the register

164 *LOTUS*, K511

Year Launched:	1961	First Owner:	T. Harcus, Orkney

Principal Dimensions:	
Length (ft)	30.9
Beam (ft)	11.6
Depth (ft)	5.3
GRT	7.13
Engine	Lister
HP	36

Lotus, K511, as *Marigold*, CT30.

History and Status:
Renamed *Andromeda* & re-registered as FR360
Renamed *Snowflake* & *Danarie*
Renamed *Marigold* & re-registered as CT30
1991: ceased fishing

165 *NORTH-FLEET*, FD226

Year Launched:	1962	First Owner:	J. Patterson, Fleetwood

Principal Dimensions:	
Length (ft)	45.0
Beam (ft)	16.0
Depth (ft)	6.0
GRT	23.0
Engine	Gardner
HP	84

North-Fleet, FD226, at Fleetwood.

History and Status:
Ceased fishing by 1997

166 *ANGELA MAY*, SH121

Year Launched:	1962	First Owner:	R. Cammish, Filey

Principal Dimensions:	
Length (ft)	29.0
Beam (ft)	9.0
Depth (ft)	
GRT	
Engine	Parsons
HP	42

The coble *Angela May*, SH121, on the beach.

History and Status:
Yorkshire coble, delivered to Filey by train and sent back by return to builder to rectify the stern, which wasn't right, before being returned to Filey by train. The only coble built by James Noble
Renamed *Jean Ann*

167 *KINDLY LIGHT*, BK168

Year Launched:	1963	First Owner:	R. Douglas, Seahouses

Principal Dimensions:	
Length (ft)	32.0
Beam (ft)	11.5
Depth (ft)	5.0
GRT	
Engine	Gardner
HP	33

Small yawl *Kindly Light*, BK168.

History and Status:
Re-registered as LK168, B63
2021: sunk during Storm Arwen in Amble harbour (November); later raised and taken on by a new owner to restore.

168 *MAUREEN*, WK270

Year Launched:	1963	First Owner:	W. Simpson, Thurso

Principal Dimensions:	
Length (ft)	55.2
Beam (ft)	17.5
Depth (ft)	6.2
GRT	24.8
Engine	Gardner
HP	150

Maureen, WK270, at Scrabster.

History and Status:
1976: renamed *Crimson Arrow 4* & re-registered as CN155
1992: re-registered as N128
2012: re-registered as OB128
2018: re-registered as KY142
2020: major restoration & renamed *Crimson Arrow*, KY142

169 *QUEST 2*, ME177

Year Launched:	1963	First Owner:	S. Morrison, Gourdon

Principal Dimensions:	
Length (ft)	33.1
Beam (ft)	12.25
Depth (ft)	4.8
GRT	8.26
Engine	Lister
HP	36

Quest 2, ME177, the outside boat, at Gourdon.

History and Status:
Re-registered as PW177, WK508

170 *ZENITH*, LK648

Year Launched:	1964	First Owner:	A. Polson, Lerwick

Principal Dimensions:	
Length (ft)	55.2
Beam (ft)	17.6
Depth (ft)	5.9
GRT	23.41
Engine	Gardner
HP	150

Zenith, LK648.

History and Status:
Re-registered as UL222

171 *AMETHYST*, LK635

Year Launched:	1964	First Owner:	D. Anderson, Lerwick

Principal Dimensions:	
Length (ft)	55.6
Beam (ft)	17.9
Depth (ft)	5.8
GRT	23.09
Engine	Gardner
HP	152

Amethyst, LK635. (Colin Hughson)

History and Status:
1980: re-registered as WK635
1985: renamed *Caledonia* & re-registered as TT34
2002: ceased fishing

172 *OUR CATHERINE*, H352

Year Launched:	1964	First Owner:	Boggs & Co., Bridlington

Principal Dimensions:	
Length (ft)	59.0
Beam (ft)	20.1
Depth (ft)	7.8
GRT	49.9
Engine	Gardner
HP	200

Our Catherine, H352, ashore.

History and Status:
Re-registered as K352
1985: sunk

173 *CONCORD*, LK657

Year Launched:	1965	First Owner:	R. Aitken, Yell

Principal Dimensions:	
Length (ft)	55.2
Beam (ft)	17.7
Depth (ft)	6.0
GRT	24.42
Engine	Kelvin
HP	180

Concord, LK657, just launched.

History and Status:
Re-registered as B92

174 *SILVER SPRAY*, FR365

Year Launched:	1965	First Owner:	A. Cardno, Fraserburgh

Principal Dimensions:	
Length (ft)	63.8
Beam (ft)	20.2
Depth (ft)	8.45
GRT	46.01
Engine	Gardner
HP	150

Silver Spray, FR365.

History and Status:
1966: wrecked on rocks off Horse Island near Ullapool and sank. Crew rescued by *The Way*

175 *INCENTIVE*, PD349

Year Launched:	1965	First Owner:	T. Hay, Peterhead

Principal Dimensions:	
Length (ft)	39.8
Beam (ft)	15.0
Depth (ft)	7.4
GRT	18.78
Engine	Gardner
HP	84

History and Status:
1987: sold to England & re-registered as SH68

176 *SWEET PROMISE*, A746

Year Launched:	1965	First Owner:	Mr Cormack, Stonehaven

Principal Dimensions:	
Length (ft)	33.5
Beam (ft)	13.3
Depth (ft)	5.5
GRT	10.53
Engine	Lister
HP	43

Sweet Promise, A746, as *Tern*, LH53.

History and Status:
Re-registered as KY26
1975: sold to England & re-registered as PH30, FY144
Renamed *Sarah of Looe*, FY144
Renamed *Tern* & re-registered as LH53

177 *HEATHER MAID*, CT81

Year Launched:	1965	First Owner:	J. Watterson, Port Erin

Principal Dimensions:	
Length (ft)	54.6
Beam (ft)	17.7
Depth (ft)	7.3
GRT	38.0
Engine	Gardner
HP	150

Heather Maid, CT81, being launched.

History and Status:
2007: changed hands from Wattersons to Billy Caley
2018: caught fire in Peel and sank
2020: scrapped at Ramsey shipyard slipway

178 *EMMA MARSHALL*

Year Launched:	1965	First Owner:	Unknown

Principal Dimensions:	
Length (ft)	56.0
Beam (ft)	16.5
Depth (ft)	8.2
GRT	50.0
Engine	Gardner
HP	150

Stern view of *Emma Marshall*.
(Maureen and Bruce Herd)

History and Status:
Built as a yacht
1972: owned by G.D.Winter, Salcombe

179 *ONWARD STAR*, SH165

Year Launched:	1966	First Owner:	Boggs & Co. Ltd, Bridlington

Principal Dimensions:	
Length (ft)	52.5
Beam (ft)	17.6
Depth (ft)	7.3
GRT	39.53
Engine	Gardner
HP	200

Onward Star, SH165, up the beach at
Scarborough for a coat of paint.

History and Status:
2021: still fishing

180 *ARGO*, FR255

Year Launched:	1966	First Owner:	R. Smith, Fraserburgh

Principal Dimensions:	
Length (ft)	64.5
Beam (ft)	20.5
Depth (ft)	8.5
GRT	46.66
Engine	Gardner
HP	200

The first transom-sterned Noble's boat *Argo*, FR255.

History and Status:
Renamed *Glenfarg*, FR255
Renamed *Splendour* & re-registered as PD964
2002: decommissioned

181 *LOCH BERVIE*, BF411

Year Launched:	1966	First Owner:	J. Watt, Macduff

Principal Dimensions:	
Length (ft)	59.8
Beam (ft)	20.3
Depth (ft)	7.5
GRT	38.71
Engine	Gardner
HP	200

Loch Bervie, BF411, moored up on the north coast of Mull.

History and Status:
1974: renamed *Little Flower* & re-registered as CY129
1979: sunk in the South Minch

182 *FAITHFUL*, BA296

Year Launched:	1966	First Owner:	F. Wiseman, Ayr

Principal Dimensions:	
Length (ft)	55.5
Beam (ft)	17.5
Depth (ft)	6.0
GRT	24.1
Engine	Kelvin
HP	180

Faithful, BA296, soon after launch.

History and Status:
1988: renamed *Golden Hope 2* & re-registered as AH84, LH384
Renamed *Agate 2* & re-registered as SY256
2002: decommissioned

183 *MARWOOD*, BA339

Year Launched:	1967	First Owner:	J. Woodman, Annan

Principal Dimensions:	
Length (ft)	39.8
Beam (ft)	16.1
Depth (ft)	6.6
GRT	17.93
Engine	Kelvin
HP	120

Marwood as *Brighter Hope*, PD113, at Peterhead. (Peter Drummond)

History and Status:
1971: re-registered as WK339
1973: renamed *Brighter Hope* & re-registered as PD113
1995: renamed *Felicity 3* & re-registered as CN393
2000: re-registered as B911
2002: decommissioned and broken up

184 *ENCHANTER*, FR408

Year Launched:	1967	First Owner:	Boggs & Co. Ltd, Bridlington

Principal Dimensions:	
Length (ft)	55.0
Beam (ft)	17.58
Depth (ft)	5.9
GRT	23.92
Engine	Gardner
HP	200

Enchanter, FR408, unloading at Bridlington.

History and Status:
1998: decommissioned

185 *CYNOSURE*, A774

Year Launched:	1967	First Owner:	D. Forsyth, Stonehaven

Principal Dimensions:	
Length (ft)	49.9
Beam (ft)	17.3
Depth (ft)	6.9
GRT	24.71
Engine	Gardner
HP	150

Cynosure, A774, at Aberdeen.

History and Status:
1979: renamed *Silver Spray 2* & re-registered as CN219
1983: re-registered as TT77
1998: re-registered as B891
2002: decommissioned and broken up

186 *GOLDSEEKER*

Year Launched:	1967	First Owner:	Department of Agriculture and Fisheries for Scotland

Principal Dimensions:	
Length (ft)	50.0
Beam (ft)	17.0
Depth (ft)	10.0
GRT	39.0
Engine	Gardner
HP	110

Goldseeker at launch without her wheelhouse. (Maureen and Bruce Herd)

History and Status:
Fishery Research Vessel
1993: sold into private ownership

187 *STRATHYRE*, FR4

Year Launched:	1968	First Owner:	J. Wiseman, Fraserburgh

Principal Dimensions:	
Length (ft)	54.7
Beam (ft)	18.3
Depth (ft)	5.9
GRT	24.39
Engine	Kelvin
HP	180

Strathyre, FR4, having pulled up a load of old wire.

History and Status:
1989: renamed *Shannon*
1995: renamed *Freedom* & re-registered as CN194
1998: ceased fishing and used as floating store at Peterhead and later moved to Stanley Burn, Burntisland
2012: reported to be in poor condition

188 *SEA HUNTER*, FR414

Year Launched:	1968	First Owner:	J. Simpson, Bridlington

Principal Dimensions:	
Length (ft)	55.0
Beam (ft)	
Depth (ft)	
GRT	31.0
Engine	Gardner
HP	230

Sea Hunter, FR414.

History and Status:
1986: sold

189 *CAROL ANNE*, SH175

Year Launched:	1968	First Owner:	T. Mainprize, Scarborough

Principal Dimensions:	
Length (ft)	59.8
Beam (ft)	19.7
Depth (ft)	8.15
GRT	40.24
Engine	Kelvin
HP	240

Carol Anne, SH175, alongside.

History and Status:
1981: renamed *Lyncean* & re-registered as KY176
1996: ceased fishing

190 *GUIDING LIGHT*, KY207

Year Launched:	1968	First Owner:	W. Dunn, Pittenweem

Principal Dimensions:	
Length (ft)	54.3
Beam (ft)	17.75
Depth (ft)	5.9
GRT	23.94
Engine	Gardner
HP	150

Guiding Light, KY207, on festival day.

History and Status:
1981: re-registered as FR437
2003: ceased fishing and reported as being converted to pleasure at Troon
2019: reported abandoned in Portugal

191 *IRIS*, FR7

Year Launched:	1968	First Owner:	A. Gibb, Fraserburgh

Principal Dimensions:	
Length (ft)	49.5
Beam (ft)	18.2
Depth (ft)	6.2
GRT	23.46
Engine	Kelvin
HP	180

History and Status:
1975: renamed *Venture*
1975: renamed *Virgo* & re-registered as OB254
2013: renamed *Stella Maris* & re-registered as PH97
2020: sold for pleasure
2022: back in her home port of Mallaig, awaiting conversion to wildlife-spotting vessel

192 *PAMELA S*, FR38

Year Launched:	1969	First Owner:	J.W. Hall, Beverley

Principal Dimensions:	
Length (ft)	55.1
Beam (ft)	18.31
Depth (ft)	5.8
GRT	25.0
Engine	
HP	

Pamela S, FR38.

History and Status:
2012: re-registered as WY38
2019: still fishing from Whitehaven

193 *OCEAN REWARD*, FR28

Year Launched:	1969	First Owner:	J. Sanderson, Bridlington

Principal Dimensions:	
Length (ft)	52.0
Beam (ft)	17.3
Depth (ft)	7.0
GRT	
Engine	Gardner
HP	200

The launch of *Ocean Reward*, FR28, in 1969.

History and Status:
2000: ceased fishing and converted for pleasure
2007: reported for sale
2019: houseboat at Bembridge, Isle of Wight

194 *PILOT US*, H45

Year Launched:	1969	First Owner:	Boggs & Co. Ltd, Bridlington

Principal Dimensions:	
Length (ft)	58.3
Beam (ft)	18.21
Depth (ft)	7.55
GRT	42.0
Engine	
HP	

Pilot Us, H45, as B145, still fishing from Ardglass.

History and Status:
1990: re-registered B145
2019: still fishing from Ardglass

195 *NEW DAWN*, FR19

Year Launched:	1969	First Owner:	T. West, Fraserburgh

Principal Dimensions:	
Length (ft)	44.4
Beam (ft)	15.8
Depth (ft)	7.5
GRT	22.4
Engine	Gardner
HP	110

New Dawn, FR19, built in the small shed at the yard.

History and Status:
1989: re-registered as PL1
1991: re-registered as OB506
1992: sunk off Rhum, August 1992

196 *LAHAI ROI*, LH18

Year Launched:	1969	First Owner:	J. Sinclair, Port Seton

Principal Dimensions:	
Length (ft)	56.0
Beam (ft)	18.3
Depth (ft)	7.5
GRT	32.3
Engine	Gardner
HP	230

Lahai Roi, LH18, the name translating literally to 'well of the living God'.

History and Status:
1990: re-registered as B118
2002: decommissioned and broken up

197 *TRUSTFUL*, A74

Year Launched:	1969	First Owner:	D. Andrew, Stonehaven

Principal Dimensions:	
Length (ft)	40.0
Beam (ft)	16.0
Depth (ft)	6.5
GRT	17.55
Engine	Gardner
HP	110

Trustful, A74, on slip at Mallaig.

History and Status:
2012: re-registered as SN12
2018: still fishing from North Shields
2020: reported for sale

198 *GOLDEN QUEST*, FR56

Year Launched:	1970	First Owner:	J. Watt, Fraserburgh

Principal Dimensions:	
Length (ft)	55.9
Beam (ft)	18.2
Depth (ft)	77.0
GRT	33.23
Engine	Gardner
HP	230

Golden Quest, FR56.

History and Status:
1977: re-registered as K397
1984: re-registered as LH23
2002: decommissioned and broken up by C.J. Marine on the River Tyne

199 *INTEGRITY*, FR40

Year Launched:	1970	First Owner:	A. Ritchie, Cairnbulg

Principal Dimensions:	
Length (ft)	40.9
Beam (ft)	16.0
Depth (ft)	6.5
GRT	17.97
Engine	Lister
HP	102

Integrity, FR40.

History and Status:
1979: re-registered as PD40
1981: ceased fishing

200 *OCEANA*, A327

Year Launched:	1970	First Owner:	C. Kennedy, Aberdeen

Principal Dimensions:	
Length (ft)	60.0
Beam (ft)	20.5
Depth (ft)	8.7
GRT	45.1
Engine	Caterpillar
HP	240

History and Status:
1974: sank in heavy weather and crew saved

201 *FAITHFUL*, INS38

Year Launched:	1970	First Owner:	A. Jack, Hopeman

Principal Dimensions:	
Length (ft)	65.5
Beam (ft)	20.5
Depth (ft)	7.5
GRT	42.62
Engine	Gardner
HP	230

Faithful, INS38

History and Status:
1995: re-registered as WK126
2002: decommissioned and broken up at Stornoway

202 *FLOREAT*, FR65

Year Launched:	1970	First Owner:	W. Duthie, Fraserburgh

Principal Dimensions:	
Length (ft)	55.0
Beam (ft)	18.2
Depth (ft)	7.5
GRT	31.88
Engine	Thornycroft
HP	164

Floreat, FR65, about to be launched.

History and Status:
1998: ceased fishing

203 *GOOD INTENT*, FR47

Year Launched:	1970	First Owner:	T. Mainprize, Scarborough

Principal Dimensions:	
Length (ft)	60.0
Beam (ft)	19.5
Depth (ft)	8.37
GRT	38.34
Engine	Volvo Penta
HP	319

History and Status:
1992: renamed *Grace* & re-registered as SH155
1996: renamed *Good Intent* & re-registered as WY470
1997: renamed *Faithful Friend 3* & re-registered as FR615
2008: struck rocks off Bayble Island, Isle of Lewis, and sank

204 *SILVER BELL*, INS52

Silver Bell, INS52.

Year Launched:	1971	First Owner:	D. Patience, Avoch

Principal Dimensions:	
Length (ft)	60.8
Beam (ft)	20.0
Depth (ft)	8.2
GRT	41.7
Engine	Gardner
HP	230

History and Status:
1986: re-registered as CN312
1989: renamed *Silver Dee* & re-registered as A63
1990: re-registered as B310
2015: collided with *Good Intent* south of Ardglass and sank

205 *EASTERN DAWN*, FR82

Eastern Morn as *Silver Quest*, AR190. (Peter Drummond)

Year Launched:	1971	First Owner:	F. Nicol, Fraserburgh

Principal Dimensions:	
Length (ft)	55.5
Beam (ft)	18.2
Depth (ft)	5.7
GRT	23.86
Engine	Gardner
HP	230

History and Status:
1985: renamed *Bon Accord* & re-registered as BF55
1990: renamed *Leandris* & re-registered as WK471
1993: renamed *Incentive* & re-registered as BA471
1995: renamed *Mysotis* & re-registered as AR190
1996: went ashore at Rhum and keel damaged: salvaged and repaired
1996: renamed *Silver Quest*, AR190
2019: still fishing from Troon

206 *VENUS*, FR79

Year Launched:	1971	First Owner:	J.G. Cole, Whitby

Principal Dimensions:	
Length (ft)	55.1
Beam (ft)	18.2
Depth (ft)	5.8
GRT	25.0
Engine	
HP	

Venus, FR79.

History and Status:
First transom-sterned boat
2006: ceased fishing and to be converted to houseboat, though not completed
2022: lying ashore by the Larpool Viaduct on the River Esk, Whitby

207 *JANN DENISE*, FR80

Year Launched:	1971	First Owner:	R. Walker, Scarborough

Principal Dimensions:	
Length (ft)	55.5
Beam (ft)	18.2
Depth (ft)	5.8
GRT	24.36
Engine	Gardner
HP	230

Jann Denise ashore. (George Westwood)

History and Status:
2021: re-registered as PL206 and based in the Isle of Man, rigged for scallops and trawling

208 *FRUITFUL HARVEST*, PD47

Year Launched:	1972	First Owner:	R. Reid, Peterhead

Principal Dimensions:	
Length (ft)	59.8
Beam (ft)	21.1
Depth (ft)	8.8
GRT	46.29
Engine	Gardner
HP	230

Fruitful Harvest, PD47 as *Press On*, BF65.

History and Status:
1979: renamed *Eastern Dawn 2*, FR82
1986: re-registered as FR182
1991: renamed *Press On* & re-registered as BF65
2011: decommissioned at Ghent

209 *EDELWEISS*, FR104

Year Launched:	1972	First Owner:	J. Goodbrand, Fraserburgh

Principal Dimensions:	
Length (ft)	54.5
Beam (ft)	18.2
Depth (ft)	5.6
GRT	23.16
Engine	Gardner
HP	230

Edelweiss, FR104, soon after launch with her shelter deck, which was later removed.

History and Status:
1972: built with engine forward and launched directly off the quay resulting in some five cracked frames which had to be replaced. No other forward engined vessels were launched this way
1999: renamed *Comrade* & re-registered as SY337
2020: still fishing from Stornoway

210 *OUR RACHEL*, FR97

Year Launched:	1972	First Owner:	C. Jenkinson, Scarborough

Principal Dimensions:	
Length (ft)	54.7
Beam (ft)	18.3
Depth (ft)	5.6
GRT	23.33
Engine	Gardner
HP	230

Our Rachel, FR97, as *Mystique*, SY89.

History and Status:
1986: renamed *Strathgarry 4* & re-registered as SY89
1989: renamed *Mystique*, SY89, based in Penzance
1995: struck Outer Buck rock and sank when outward bound from Newlyn. Crew rescued

211 *SILVER GEM*, INS61

Year Launched:	1972	First Owner:	W. Jack, Avoch

Principal Dimensions:	
Length (ft)	60.0
Beam (ft)	19.6
Depth (ft)	8.01
GRT	40.01
Engine	Gardner
HP	230

Silver Gem as BF27. (Peter Drummond)

History and Status:
1981: re-registered as CN297
1984: re-registered as BF27
2001: renamed *Ocean Wanderer* & re-registered as FR942
2002: decommissioned and broken up

212 *SILVER SPRAY*, OB140

Year Launched:	1972	First Owner:	D. Kirkpatrick, Mull

Principal Dimensions:	
Length (ft)	39.7
Beam (ft)	16.1
Depth (ft)	6.6
GRT	17.69
Engine	Gardner
HP	110

Silver Spray, OB140, leaving the tidal lock at Crinan Basin.

History and Status:
2016: ceased fishing

213 *CRIMOND 2*, KY246

Year Launched:	1973	First Owner:	W. Boyter, Pittenweem

Principal Dimensions:	
Length (ft)	54.8
Beam (ft)	18.2
Depth (ft)	5.6
GRT	23.46
Engine	Gardner
HP	230

Crimond 2, KY246, alongside at Pittenweem.

History and Status:
1989: sold to Cornwall
1996: sold to Scarborough
2001: sank 30 miles from Scarborough after vessel flooded, two crew rescued

214 *DEWY ROSE*, FR144

Year Launched:	1973	First Owner:	J. Mitchell, Sandhaven

Principal Dimensions:	
Length (ft)	58.9
Beam (ft)	20.1
Depth (ft)	8.6
GRT	43.02
Engine	Kelvin
HP	240

Dewy Rose, FR144, leaving Fraserburgh.

History and Status:
1999: re-registered as B901
2004: decommissioned and broken up at Kilkeel

215 *DUTHIES*, FR132

Year Launched:	1973	First Owner:	L. Duthie, Fraserburgh

Principal Dimensions:	
Length (ft)	43.8
Beam (ft)	16.0
Depth (ft)	7.0
GRT	20.66
Engine	Gardner
HP	152

Duthies, FR132.

History and Status:
1986: renamed *Silver Fern* & re-registered CN75
1990: re-registered as TT175
1998: re-registered as B889
2017: re-registered as MT99
2019: still fishing from Maryport

216 *VALIANT 2*, FR117

Valiant 2, FR117.

Year Launched:	1973	First Owner:	D. Sim, Fraserburgh

Principal Dimensions:	
Length (ft)	55.3
Beam (ft)	18.3
Depth (ft)	5.6
GRT	23.7
Engine	Gardner
HP	230

History and Status:
1980: renamed *Five Sisters* & re-registered as OB353
1995: renamed *Aurora* & re-registered as CY463
1998: renamed *Primrose* & re-registered as FR233, TT233, CY793
2002: renamed *Supreme* & re-registered as HL10
2011: re-registered as B1004
2013: renamed *Diamond D* & re-registered as SN100
2020: capsized & sank 18 miles off the Tyne after landing a large boulder. Crew of two rescued by Tyne lifeboat

217 *NICOLA SUZANNE*, FR141

Year Launched:	1974	First Owner:	M. Anderson, Scarborough

Principal Dimensions:	
Length (ft)	51.5
Beam (ft)	17.0
Depth (ft)	5.7
GRT	24.0
Engine	
HP	

Nicola Suzanne, as *Radiant Morn*, FR141.

History and Status:
1986: renamed *Radiant Morn*, FR141
2019: still fishing from Campbeltown

218 *SERENE*, PD58

Year Launched:	1974	First Owner:	J. Duncan, Peterhead

Principal Dimensions:	
Length (ft)	39.8
Beam (ft)	15.7
Depth (ft)	7.0
GRT	18.45
Engine	Gardner
HP	152

Serene, PD58. (Peter Drummond)

History and Status:
1998: ceased fishing

219 *HARVEST REAPER*, FR177

Year Launched:	1974	First Owner:	Unknown

Principal Dimensions:	
Length (ft)	55.8
Beam (ft)	18.2
Depth (ft)	5.7
GRT	24.51
Engine	Kelvin
HP	280

Jimmy May's *Harvest Reaper*, FR177, just launched.

History and Status:
1998: re-registered as TT177
2012: re-registered as PW177
2020: reported for sale

220 *HARVESTER*, PD98

Year Launched:	1974	First Owner:	R. Stephen, Boddam

Principal Dimensions:	
Length (ft)	39.5
Beam (ft)	16.0
Depth (ft)	7.2
GRT	
Engine	Gardner
HP	150

Harvester, PD98.

History and Status:
1982: sold to England & re-registered as F98
1986: re-registered as FH198
2019: still fishing from Bridlington

221 *PATHFINDER*, FR172

Year Launched:	1974	First Owner:	T. & R. Mainprize, Scarborough

Principal Dimensions:	
Length (ft)	62.0
Beam (ft)	
Depth (ft)	
GRT	44
Engine	Gardner
HP	2 × 230

Pathfinder, FR172, at Scarborough.

History and Status:
1978: sunk when catch shifted off Hartlepool (6 December)

222 *GOLDEN FLEECE*, KY116

Year Launched:	1975	First Owner:	R. Duncan, St Andrews

Principal Dimensions:	
Length (ft)	45.5
Beam (ft)	16.1
Depth (ft)	7.1
GRT	21.66
Engine	Caterpillar
HP	190

Golden Fleece, KY116. (Darren Purves)

History and Status:
1995: re-registered as FH206
2009: re-registered as MT99
2015: re-registered as N185
2020: still fishing from Kilkeel

223 *IRIS*, FR188

Year Launched:	1975	First Owner:	A. Gibb, Fraserburgh

Principal Dimensions:	
Length (ft)	55.1
Beam (ft)	18.1
Depth (ft)	57
GRT	24.28
Engine	Kelvin
HP	280

Iris as *Cavina*, BF33.

History and Status:
1985: renamed *Cavina* & re-registered as BF33
1996: renamed *Arrivian* & re-registered as WY170
1997: renamed *Arrivian 2* & re-registered as E485
2002: renamed *Nicholas M* & re-registered as WY485
2007: renamed *Freedom* & re-registered as CN111
2020: still fishing from Oban

224 *FRUITFUL HARVEST 3*, PD247

Year Launched:	1976	First Owner:	R. Reid, Peterhead

Principal Dimensions:	
Length (ft)	65.0
Beam (ft)	21.9
Depth (ft)	7.9
GRT	47.99
Engine	Gardner
HP	230

Fruitful Harvest 3 with shelter deck additions.

History and Status:
2008: re-registered as GY991
2017: ceased fishing and being converted as a live aboard in Wales

225 *OUR HERITAGE*, FR237

Year Launched:	1976	First Owner:	C. Jenkinson, Scarborough

Principal Dimensions:	
Length (ft)	53.5
Beam (ft)	18.0
Depth (ft)	5.2
GRT	22.0
Engine	Kelvin
HP	375

Our Heritage, FR237, rigged for scallop dredging. (Peter Drummond)

History and Status:
Early 1990s: sold to Maryport, then Welsh owners, then Oban
2015: reported scalloping out of Kirkcudbright
2012: still fishing out of Maryport under registry MT127

226 *OCEAN HARVESTER*, N273

Year Launched:	1976	First Owner:	T. Maginnis, Kilkeel

Principal Dimensions:	
Length (ft)	72.0
Beam (ft)	
Depth (ft)	
GRT	41.0
Engine	
HP	500

Ocean Harvester, N273.

History and Status:
Hull built in the Halso yard, Sweden, and fitted out by James Noble when Swedish yard closed due to bankruptcy

227 *DUTCH BANK*, K292

Dutch Bank, K292, as *Brighter Morn*, CY77. (Peter Drummond)

Year Launched:	1976	First Owner:	J. McIntosh, Orkney

Principal Dimensions:	
Length (ft)	56.0
Beam (ft)	19.0
Depth (ft)	6.0
GRT	24.0
Engine	Gardner
HP	230

History and Status:
Initial job from J. Anderson (Boatbuilders) Ltd of Stromness, until they passed into receivership and Noble's took over
1985: re-registered as UL56
1989: renamed *Brighter Morn 2*, UL56
2000: re-registered as SY33
2008: re-registered as CY77

228 *INDEPENDENCE*, FR196

Independence at
launch, the only
vessel not launched
into Balaclava Basin.
(Fred Normandale)

Year Launched:	1977	First Owner:	F. Normandale, Scarborough

Principal Dimensions:	
Length (ft)	58.75
Beam (ft)	20.1
Depth (ft)	7.97
GRT	39.07
Engine	Kelvin
HP	240

History and Status:
2012: re-registered as SH196
2013: re-registered as OB196
2019: fishing from Mallaig

229 *DEVOTION*, PD217

Year Launched:	1978	First Owner:	A. Strachan, Peterhead

Principal Dimensions:	
Length (ft)	74.7
Beam (ft)	21.7
Depth (ft)	6.8
GRT	46.88
Engine	Kelvin
HP	490

Devotion, PD217.

History and Status:
2002: collided with pair trawling partner *Fruitful Bough* 150 miles east of Aberdeen when both were heading for fishing grounds. Crew rescued (24 June)

230 *SCORESBY*, FR264

Year Launched:	1978	First Owner:	T. Bennison, Whitby

Principal Dimensions:	
Length (ft)	56.4
Beam (ft)	18.0
Depth (ft)	7.8
GRT	24.72
Engine	Kelvin
HP	375

Scoresby as *Rebekah Jayne*, OB235.
(Peter Drummond)

History and Status:
1991: renamed *Lead Us Forth* & re-registered WY235
1994: renamed *Jacqueline Louise*
2002: renamed *Christina*
2008: renamed *Rebekah Jayne* & re-registered as OB235
2019: still fishing from Campbeltown

231 *ROSEBAY*, PD313

Rosebay, PD313.

Year Launched:	1979	First Owner:	W. Lawson, Peterhead

Principal Dimensions:	
Length (ft)	52.75
Beam (ft)	17.4
Depth (ft)	
GRT	24.12
Engine	Gardner
HP	

History and Status:
Re-registered as PD65
1988: renamed *Progress* & re-registered as BF1
Re-registered as FR103
1997: re-registered as BF820
2008: renamed *Maryeared* & re-registered as TT57
2015: renamed *Progress* & re-registered as AR871
2020: still fishing from Troon

232 *WISTARIA 2*, FR263

Year Launched:	1979	First Owner:	A. Cowe, Fraserburgh

Principal Dimensions:	
Length (ft)	75.6
Beam (ft)	21.7
Depth (ft)	7.0
GRT	49.42
Engine	Kelvin
HP	660

Wistaria 2, FR263, just launched.

History and Status:
1989: re-registered as B240
1998: moved to Mallaig
2000: flooded and sank 4 miles south-east of Barra. Crew rescued

233 *ASPIRE*, LK239

Year Launched:	1980	First Owner:	A. Smith, Burra

Principal Dimensions:	
Length (ft)	57.0
Beam (ft)	18.3
Depth (ft)	8.4
GRT	36.17
Engine	Kelvin
HP	300

Aspire, LK239, as *Stella Maris*, CY250.

History and Status:
2008: renamed *Stella Maris* & re-registered as CY250
2021: still fishing from Gairloch

234 *PISCEAN*, FR276

Year Launched:	1980	First Owner:	L. Mainprize, Scarborough

Principal Dimensions:	
Length (ft)	65.5
Beam (ft)	21.5
Depth (ft)	8.2
GRT	48.47
Engine	Kelvin
HP	495

Piscean, FR276, in Scarborough.

History and Status:
1986: renamed *Chrysolite*
2002: renamed *Chrisamie*, FR276
2004: flooded and sank 100 miles north-east of Aberdeen. Crew saved

235 *MARGARET JANE*, FR297

Year Launched:	1980	First Owner:	R. Mainprize, Scarborough

Principal Dimensions:	
Length (ft)	68.5
Beam (ft)	21.7
Depth (ft)	7.4
GRT	46.61
Engine	Caterpillar
HP	520

Invitation to launch ceremony.

History and Status:
1991: renamed *Scoresby* & re-registered as WY237
2000: sank in the North Sea, east of Shetland

236 *JASPER 2*, PD174

Year Launched:	1981	First Owner:	G. Forman, Peterhead

Principal Dimensions:	
Length (ft)	59.3
Beam (ft)	21.5
Depth (ft)	9.7
GRT	49.83
Engine	Kelvin
HP	280

Jasper 2, PD174, the last Noble-built vessel.

History and Status:
1992: re-registered as BK7
1997: renamed *Guiding Star* & re-registered as FR897
1999: renamed *Renown* & re-registered as LK37
2003: sold to Padstow
2007: sold to Whitehaven
2010: re-registered as N336
2014: re-registered as MT100
2018: re-registered as SN199
2019: ceased fishing

Note

Some ferries, yachts, at least two banana barges and possibly some small yawls are excluded from this list because details are not known. Furthermore, the fishing vessels listed here, where no details have been added, are probably yawls.

A Final Note

It has been fascinating collecting information and talking to family members and listening to their recollections of the yard. And, of course, it has been enjoyable talking to Bobby Jones about his memories of his times working in both yards. But memories fade and I have the constant impression that I am, in reality, a decade too late. Nevertheless, I guess that 'late is better than never'! Is it though?

As is usual when trying to collect data on vessels over 50 years old (some over a century old), we stumble across inconsistencies. One was the *Girl Jean* that

The small yawl *Breadwinner*, PD163, in her former days.

records show was built by both Wilson and James Noble. After much debate, I came to the conclusion that she was a Wilson Noble vessel, but I could be wrong. I did persevere a bit longer on this vessel, largely because I came across the boat, renamed *Shepherd Boy*, in Anglesey, where I used to live, before she was finally put to rest.

I was similarly alerted to the small yawl *Breadwinner* lying at Boddam so, on my circumnavigation of northern Scotland, I just had to drop by. From earlier photos she looked in great form but I was saddened to see she had fallen into disrepair. However, she clearly had the remains of her registration PD163 painted on her foredeck and an RSS number A13219 carved into her main beam. Websites point to her having been built in Fraserburgh in 1932, but I was unable to find any record of this. As she is a small yawl, it is possible that she was not documented. With 1932 being the year that James Noble set up shop, maybe he built her on spec. On the other hand, maybe she is another of Wilson Noble's unrecorded vessels. Nevertheless, we are left with a boat, and no definite proof of her provenance. Maybe that will unearth itself in time, as maybe many other pointers I might have missed will do. I can only apologise for any omissions or errors that I did not spot at the time.

Breadwinner, perhaps even *Edith*, PD163, at Boddam in June 2021.

Fertility, PD267, showing off her great shape. She has been described as 'a proper seiner'.

Brighter Morn, CN151 (ex-*Nimrod* LH50), hauling in after seining.

Rose, INS39, showing off the shape of her stern.

Incentive, KY343
(ex-*Caberfeidh*, BRD343),
at Pittenweem, with Ian
Bowman, Sandy Brown
& Charlie Bowman on
deck. Note the difference
in stern shape from *Rose*.

Appendix

Noble Boatbuilders and the Noble and McDonald Family Tree

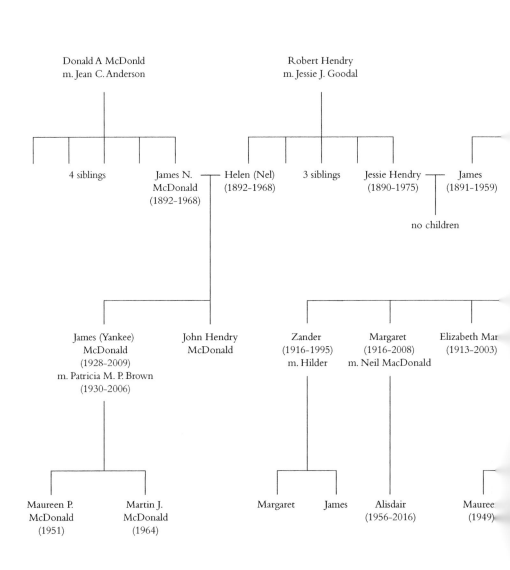

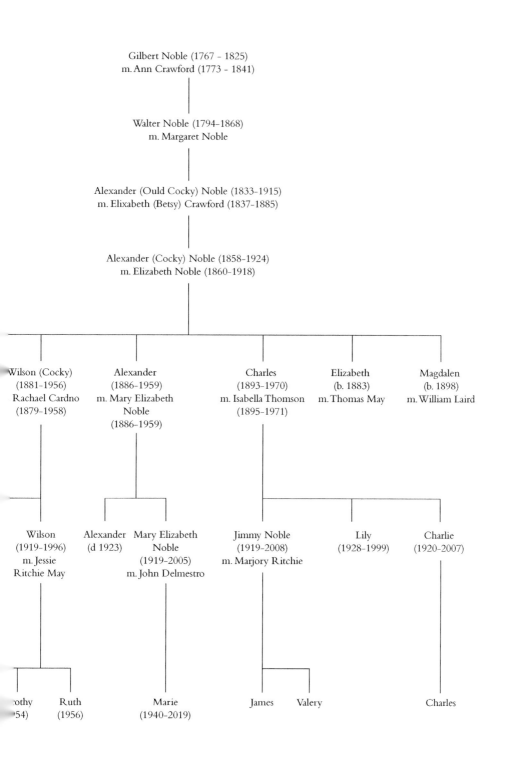

Gilbert Noble (1767 - 1825)
m. Ann Crawford (1773 - 1841)

Walter Noble (1794–1868)
m. Margaret Noble

Alexander (Ould Cocky) Noble (1833-1915)
m. Elixabeth (Betsy) Crawford (1837-1885)

Alexander (Cocky) Noble (1858-1924)
m. Elizabeth Noble (1860-1918)

Wilson (Cocky)
(1881-1956)
Rachael Cardno
(1879-1958)

Alexander
(1886-1959)
m. Mary Elizabeth
Noble
(1886-1959)

Charles
(1893-1970)
m. Isabella Thomson
(1895-1971)

Elizabeth
(b. 1883)
m. Thomas May

Magdalen
(b. 1898)
m. William Laird

Wilson
(1919-1996)
m. Jessie
Ritchie May

Alexander
(d 1923)

Mary Elizabeth
Noble
(1919-2005)
m. John Delmestro

Jimmy Noble
(1919-2008)
m. Marjory Ritchie

Lily
(1928-1999)

Charlie
(1920-2007)

othy
54)

Ruth
(1956)

Marie
(1940-2019)

James

Valery

Charles

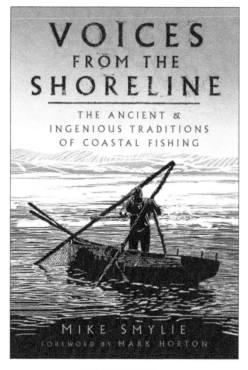

978 0 7509 9755 3

'Ultimately, [this] meditative, lachrymose work brings to life an era when humans took enough to sustain their needs, before industrial-scale operations swept in and mechanically swept up so much of the sea's resources that the old ways were hung out to dry. Is the lesson, therein, that we should cherish the recording of past lives and past work – and if so, how?'

Simon Hacker,
Stroud Times

FROM THE SAME AUTHOR

978 0 7509 9219 0

'With over 160 photographs of wooden boats, many of which have not been published before, [this] … book recording the history of the renowned Fraserburgh boatbuilder Thomas Summers & Co. Ltd will appeal to both boat enthusiasts and historians.'

David Linkie,
Fishing News UK